Life in Cardigans

Life in Cardigans

Val Fraser

Inhousemedia

Published by inhousemedia.

ISBN 978-0-9935749-0-0

Cover photo: Courtesy of the author

Introduction

I hope you will be pleased to find a little bit of yourself, or someone you love, within this collection of stories. And that in doing so you will know yourself a little better, love yourself a little more and feel more at home in your own cardigan.

Val Fraser

Contents

1 Beginnings

"She has no fear of winter for her household, for she has made warm clothes for all of them." Proverbs 31:21 The Living Bible.

Why nannas knit

"Alexander Fleming Miss, it was Alexander Fleming." My numbed hand was finally released from the vertical position it was locked into, dropping down heavily by my side. Welcome blood returned to the ends of my fingers. "That's correct" she said with obvious disbelief "Alexander Fleming is credited with discovering Penicillin, and how exactly do you know this?"

"Because my mum told me that I nearly died when I was two weeks old and it was Fleming's Penicillin that saved my life."

According to the Met Office archive, in the month I was born a cyclone moved southward from the Norwegian Sea, and as cold air spread over England, temperatures dropped to 10° Fahrenheit equating to minus 12° Celsius. I was just eight days old.

The little house where I was born lay deep in the heart of 'bronchitis country'. With just one coal fire to heat the whole place it must have been pretty chilly. By the age of two weeks I was taken into hospital suffering from life threatening double bronchial pneumonia "and nearly died" so the family folklore goes.

My Dad told me the tale of him frantically cycling many miles to the hospital to see me. As I'm writing this the realisation that he was a young man faced with the very real possibility of losing his new born baby daughter hits me. He must have been terrified, freezing cold and feeling very alone. For the first time ever the depth of his personal anguish dawns on me and the tears roll readily down my face. Dad is gone now, but I remember how he hated the cold with a vengeance. I'm finally starting to understand why. I've often wondered if that frightened young man struck a deal for my life with his God that night because I've always sensed his presence with me. Deep seated awkwardness made me too cowardly to ever ask such a daft question.

Does extreme cold, severe enough to kill a baby, feed the primal force which causes mums, aunties and nannas to knit? Does a matriarchal sense of protection for the life of a new born transpose itself into a garment which can offer warmth and security from a very real threat? And can any heart resist melting with broodiness at the sight of a beautiful cardigan lovingly crafted in anticipation of the arrival of a precious little one?

Owing to my sickly start in life I've always felt the cold sharply; can't muster enough puff to sing a decent note or blow up a balloon for toffee. But from that day to this I've rarely been seen without a lovely warm cardigan. Surviving being born in comparatively tough conditions can be credited in no small part to Alexander Fleming and my parent's diligence in seeking medical assistance. I like to think my father's prayer played a part too.

Peaches and cream

"What with the car picking me up so early and all I didn't take my tablets today" she reasoned as her trembling hand reached for a fibrous triangle of white bread. The familiar smile flickered briefly over her fragile white skin straining wearily towards the outer corner of her right eye, before dropping quickly down again, as if the effort against gravity were too great to sustain it for long. We sat drinking tea balancing our little cups on too-small-saucers, watching the men folk with envy. Strong shoulders upon which the smooth, golden oak had rested briefly were awkwardly confined in Persil white shirts and coal black suits. Because or in spite of them, they were standing taller and straighter than usual, and enthusiastically downing huge pints of swirling, creamy black Guinness.

My reading was OK, I think. I didn't understand it all but I felt sure it brought comfort to them. That's what matters today and I'm honoured to have taken part. "Treasure your memories" the priest warmly implored us from behind the coldness of his stone table. "Keep them in your heart" he added with a softly questioning up lift. A brief search through my mind's archive opened a distant memory of my lovely auntie with her Camay girl complexion and vintage style. As it played in my mind's eye I could see her smile flickering a little brighter then, and the firm steadiness of those now shaking, widowed hands.

Back then I felt sure that no humble paper bag had ever embraced such wonderful contents before. Her promise to me wasn't empty and my fidgety, impatient wait was over. Smiling widely in anticipation, her delicate fingers disappeared inside the bag, barely disturbing its worn edges. With one slow, smooth movement she slid out her offering, revealing it with the combined reverence and delight of a midwife bringing new life into the world.

For a moment the surprising zing of peachy warmth embraced the creaminess of her hand like a good friend. The creation that lay before me was the most beautiful piece of human art work I had ever seen in my entire life. An experience spanning all of seven years. Vibrant orange threads of wool chased this way and that, playfully winding their way along invisible paths, forming intricate, pleasing patterns. Vertical rows of deep cable stitch furrowed the front, mesmerising my young mind with the complexity and richness of their song. Cute little cuffs completed the sleeves. A single domed button nestled safely within the delicate stitches of a fine loop like a stone set in the royal ring of a fairy princess. My moist blinking eyes watched the light spin out from its pearly translucence in silvery, dancing rays. The whole thing was exquisite and magical. My second best doll loved it and would wear it always.

And right then I decided somewhere in the kitchen of my soul that cardigans were not about the pragmatic need to be clothed, nor merely the avoidance of undress. Indeed, cardigans were born of determined hands working hard to provide life-giving warmth while vanquishing killer cold. Cardigans were protection, survival, creativity, perseverance, craft and love all sharing the same moment in time. Cardigans were art you could live in and love that could go with you always.

I left my auntie sipping her tea with mourning sons and friends, treasuring in my heart her gift of love to my second best doll and that little girl who used to be me.

Red army

Grandma's kitchen stretched across the back of the house, barring four feet which the council had sliced off to install an indoor bathroom. Four clawed feet supported a roll top bath with rust stained enamel where two clumsy brass taps had dribbled hard water like tea pots with short spouts. A lavatory, as we called it, occupied the remaining couple of feet. The mysterious ceiling height cupboard towering at the foot of the bath begged a sneaky investigation. Red and blue billiard balls nested upon a towel, which nosey children were not allowed to play with. On the wall next to the toilet the head of a six inch nail protruded dangerously upwards at a 45° angle, roughly torn sheets of newspaper were impaled upon it. "When it comes to recycling paper, old folks like to cut out the middle man" winked Mum.

An under stairs pantry occupied one corner of the kitchen, a shelved grotto housing packets of pale dried peas, barley, semolina and beef dripping. Grandma's glazed caramel mixing bowl crouched squat upon the high shelf like a chunky mountain fortress protecting a precious loaf of bread tucked neatly round with a chequered blue tea towel.

There were no toys or books in the house so for fun we would go out to play in the brick walled yard. A riven faced stone path ran under the washing line, separating a scrubby lawn. Skipping up and down the path we would stop when we found a loose paving 'flag' and rock back and forth. Red ants would swarm out of their hiding place in confusion, like a tiny army displaced by enemy invasion. A select platoon of brave soldiers would scale up summer sandals, over crisp white ankle socks onto skinny ankles, inflicting wounds though minor, enough to send little girls crying into the house.

Grandma Kitty was widowed long before I was born. She was the only grandparent I knew, but I didn't really know her well. Grownups didn't have conversations with children then, and when she did speak it was in the broad dialect of the Lancashire mills which completely foxed me. It wasn't until the telling and re-telling of family stories that I got to know her. You can learn a lot about a person's character through what they spend their money on, especially when they have so little.

In spite of extreme poverty Kitty somehow managed to pay for my Dad, her son, to have music lessons and a piano accordion. Long after her death he would refer to her surprising sacrifice. And when a door to door artist sold the idea of a coloured pastel drawing of her three sons, each image exactly copied from separate photos, she scraped up the cash to buy it. The framed drawing hung proudly above her dining table for years before taking its place in my parent's home, and then mine.

Grandma would sigh knowingly: "Eeee child, you've made your bed, y'mon lie on it" meaning "You've made your choice, you must live with it." She looks at me warmly from the shelf these days; I hope I did a good job of helping to care for her son in the confusion of his winter years. Perhaps it was a family likeness and her ring on my finger which sometimes caused him to mistake me for Kitty.

In the four generations line up of my parent's musty monochrome wedding photo, which I've looked at all my life, I notice for the first time ever, that among the formal jackets and dresses Grandma is the only guest wearing a cardigan. I lean in to the photo and listen hard, straining with the ears of my soul to remember any pearls of wisdom she might posthumously offer up to me now. Looking into her small bespectacled eyes I think I catch her whisper: "Eeee child, you've made your book, y'mon put me in it!"

The girl in the wrong dress

"It's boiling in here! Take it off now child - before you pass out!" she insisted

Half glazed walls built of thin cardboard and thick glass topped off with a flat metal roof cranked up the moderate heat of an English summer's day to sweltering, desert conditions. Surrounding black tarmac absorbed the heat and radiated it back up onto the shed in the playground which passed for a classroom. Plump cheeks were flushed red. Wet snakes of hair stuck to foreheads and napes of necks. Long white socks were pushed down to ankles. Thick blazers then cardigans were slung redundantly onto backs of chairs. School ties were gingerly loosened with shifty sideways glances. Pleated fans fashioned from lined paper began to wave here and there.

Knee length V-necked sleeveless tunics cruelly set apart us first year students. Known as gymslips or pinafore dresses their scratchy hard wearing gabardine fabric necessitated the wearing of a silky petticoat or under-slip. By order, the gymslip had to be firmly belted around the waist where a kipper tie knot secured a striped woven sash, called a girdle, which was neither a tie nor a belt. A white school shirt, school tie, navy blue cardigan, blazer and a felted cloche hat, befitting of a Downton Abbey maid completed the compulsory ensemble. A look not fully appreciated by fashion conscious girls.

Along with much of my hand-me-down wardrobe, my hand-me-down gymslip so obviously pre-dated the war. Its antiquity was authenticated by me alone. The never-before-seen square neckline stood out from the V-necklines worn by all the other girls. The whole style of it seemed to bellow 'not new'. This advertisement of poverty reinforced my deeply ingrained sense of worthlessness. It shouted I'm different from you. And by different I mean not as posh, not as proper, not as good.

And for my fragile, lonely, desperate-to-belong, adolescent heart, that voice was unbearably loud and had to be silenced. By a cardigan. Which I would wear every day. No matter what the weather. No matter if the teacher ordered me to take it off.

My temperature soared with her insistent bark and the waiting eyes of my peers. The start of the lesson was halted by my refusal to comply. 'Miss' left her post at the front of the classroom and began stomping through the ranks circling towards me from behind. The vigorous rolling up of her sleeves indicated to me that she was about to physically wrench the cardigan off me. A drama I was anxious to avoid. In a heated panic I quickly took the cardigan off. And clearly, everyone could see that this girl was wearing the wrong dress.

Having little perspective on life and no frame of reference to work from I couldn't analyse the situation, I could only experience it for the intense, burning, moment of shame that it was.

Whispers rustled around the room and I knew they were talking about me. A simmering distrust of school teachers, however well meaning, was born. A thing for cardigans and an acid wit were enlisted for the job of protecting my bare, cardigan-less, heart.

2 Motion

"The family, that dear octopus from whose tentacles we never quite escape nor, in our innermost hearts, ever quite wish to." Dodie Smith, English novelist and playwright 1896-1990.

The posh cardigan

Summer day trips to see Uncle Harold and Auntie Betty were a see-saw of excitement and boredom. The stuffy car journey lasted an age. Like brass nipples on an oak banister rail rudely punctuating the fun of a downward slide, my exhilaration was interrupted at frequent intervals with bouts of unpleasant car sickness. The smooth straightness of the motorway was avoided on the grounds of its pure evil, even on a Sunday, and our preferred route always took the sick-making, A-road which crossed over the old toll bridge.

Warburton Toll Bridge traverses the Manchester Ship Canal. It would cost my Dad two shillings and sixpence for a one way ticket or five shillings for a return. Remarkably this amount has never increased since the decimalisation of the 1970s. It remains locked in another era, much like the quaint little shelter in the middle of the road into which payment must be handed, in actual cash money. The two shillings and sixpence ticket, equating to 12.5p was rounded down to 12p and the five shilling ticket became 25p. It currently costs more to buy a return than two singles, giving the jokey impression that returning home is not such a good idea.

The whole journey was travelled along winding country lanes. We would often stop by the side of the road on the way there while I threw up my Cornflakes in the grass. On the way home we would stop on the opposite side of the road while I threw up my dinner. Mum would spit on her cotton handkerchief and wipe my mouth before stuffing it back up her sleeve and reinstalling a wobbly little me in the car. I still travel with all the resilience of a ripe banana.

Nothing says the 'Cheshire set' quite like the aroma of a coal fuelled Aga stove roasting a chicken in the kitchen. Except perhaps a grand entrance hallway lined with glossy wooden Parquet floor tiles laid in a perfect Herringbone pattern. Much parental admiration and drooling centred around the expensive parquet flooring which was quite magnificent and could be appreciated even by a tiny little girl.

Auntie Betty was a great cook and always made more food than we could eat. After Sunday lunch, or dinner as we called it, the grownups would sit and talk. My sister and I, dressed in our best summer frocks and hand knitted cardigans, would be instructed to play Monopoly with our thinky, non-biological, surrogate cousins. We were sent to play in a very hot room called the sun lounge which overlooked Uncle Harold's gently sloping garden. Monopoly is a suffocating indoor board game which I struggled to understand and quickly grew to loathe. Sitting still was torture especially when the sun was shining, there were daisy chains to be made and the garden swing beckoned playfully in the gentle breeze.

Our most exciting visit happened when the pet Goldfish, Norman, died and was dramatically resurrected before our very eyes. Norman was floating motionless on top of the water in the fish bowl. Uncle Harold scooped the dead fish out of the bowl with a tablespoon which he then preceded to fill with neat Irish Brandy. We cheered as Norman miraculously came back to life. He began happily splashing about in the spoon of Brandy, with the sheer joy of being alive, we naively deduced.

Uncle Harold lived to a 'good age' and when he died we were very sad. He was a smiling friendly man who was a good friend to my parents and always looked as if he'd just arrived home from a jolly good holiday abroad, which he may well have done because according to my Dad "they weren't short of a bob or two".

Auntie Betty was left alone with her Aga and Parquet flooring. My aging Mum and Dad made the journey over Warburton Bridge to visit her now and then. She would chat with Mum while Dad did a few odd jobs around the house and garden. As a reward for this help Auntie Betty bequeathed him Uncle Harold's 'good' cardigan. This was a substantial, masculine construction, entirely befitting of a Cheshire gentleman. Two brown suede panels covered the whole front and matching suede patches graced the elbows. The panels appeared to be inlaid into the cardigan, the remainder of which was a chunky broad ribbed knit with deep secure cuffs and a finer rib stitching to the collar, sleeves, waist and side pockets.

With a knowing sideways nod Dad patted the suede panels with a sharp bounce of his fingers and confided how it would have "cost a bob or two". Then he would wear it for painting the fence panels.

Ladies in waiting

Unfounded yet enthusiastic rumours about the French teacher's formal title were rife. Based upon the merest whisper we would secretly embellish these rumours to a ridiculous degree then pass them on. Miss Smale soon became Lady Elizabeth De Quincy Smale of Normandy, but we weren't mean to her, in fact, we were surprisingly respectful. However, the reputation of Miss Bannister, the Maths Mistress, was conclusive. The old girl was definitely the sister of Roger Bannister, of four minute mile fame, as she could stride the length of the school corridors faster than most of us youngsters. This was to be the sum total of my experience with what I perceived as the upper classes, until I moved away.

My 'digs' comprised of a single room in a modest bungalow. The owner was a horsey old girl straight out of a boarding school story book. I imagined her growing up in a stately home, addressing her parents as Mother and Father, and having midnight feasts with her 'chums'. She was totally unfazed by the invasion of this unworldly, uncultured northern girl into her home. To some degree her friendliness towards me was partially wasted because I was much more interested in boys at that time. Yet I thought her adorable and I was astounded by her trust in me when she went away for a few days and left me alone in her house as if I were an actual adult.

I gathered up the post from behind the front door and put it on the kitchen table as instructed. All the letters were addressed to 'Lady Brandwood'. I was staying in the home of a bona fide Lady. Ooooh now this was interesting! The shabby little bungalow was not at all how I expected a Lady to live. Her modest house took on new intrigue as the realisation dawned on me that everything in it belonged to a member of the upper class. I wondered if any of her possessions had come from the grand stately home I imagined her to have grown up in.

Upon her return home I took more notice of her appearance now that I knew she was a real live Lady. I had never met a Lady, or had a conversation with one, let alone shared their home. Her face has left me now but her kindness has not. Always jolly and polite she bounced around the bungalow in a heavy pleated skirt and a long knitted Aran cardigan even on warm days. Degrees of buttoning up were variable as was the wearing of what I naively presumed to be a pure silk neck scarf painstakingly woven by an elite squad of pedigree silk worms somewhere in the deepest Orient.

I deduced from my new observations, in regard to the immovable Aran cardigan, that I was clearly wrong about the stately home. Obviously My Lady, as I came to think of her, had grown up within the thick walls of a cold Scottish castle by the side of a still black lake. The Aran cardigan must have been custom knitted on the instructions of her Governess who needed her to concentrate more during Geography lessons. The fire in the draughty old study was never lit and as a young lady she was often very cold and couldn't concentrate properly. Her hands would become too cold to grasp a pencil, her mind would shut down and she struggled to complete her written assignments. Matters were no better in the warm summer months because she was often distracted by a handsome boy playing cricket outside the window and would forget to bring her books to the lesson.

Clearly the kindly Governess, who was firm but fair, instructed a local Fisherman's wife to knit the cardigan with pockets deep enough to warm both hands with comfort and house two school books in each one. The Fisherman's wife was very skilled and crafted the intricate pattern over several months. More than seven thousand stitches in all. And henceforth the cardigan kept my Lady warm, housed her school books, improved her concentration and saved her from the Governess's disapproval. When the bookish Governess inevitably died of gout and a broken heart, as all the best Governesses normally do, her lonely young student pledged never to remove the cardigan from that day to this.

When I complimented the cardigan she threw back her head and enthused with a loud horsey laugh: "Oh I do so love a good cardigan" and thrusting both her hands down into the pockets with forceful glee she added: "especially ones with good deep pockets."

The cardigan I couldn't afford

"Do you know where you're going to?"

Those song lyrics poured down from the hazy Victorian glass roof of Makinson's Shopping Arcade like the piercing voice of God in a silent wilderness. Unable to escape from them, the hard questions drenched my lonely, searching soul to the point of total saturation. Australia was a very long way from Wigan, which was most of its appeal. I clutched the travel brochure aware that, in every possible sense, I didn't have a clue where I was going.

I got as far as the south coast of England. An overwhelming sense of freedom engulfed me and the staggering beauty of the landscape readily welcomed my hope-starved soul. The food was wonderful but money was tight. Selfish teenage pursuits quite rightly consumed my life and I rarely thought of home. Until Christmas.

I had no idea how to express my love for my parents, or that the expression of my love for them was something which was even a possibility. I'd never really seen this done in a direct way by anyone in real life. The love between us was not the easily spoken kind, for it was mined too far down in the deep unreachable gritty seams of belligerent assumption. Love was never communicated in spoken words, implied or otherwise. This silence ruled to such an extent that you could have believed it was forbidden by law to speak of such things. The red cheeked farmer's wife for whom I worked delivering milk as a girl once asked me "Are you a close family?" Stupidly mirroring her exaggerated nods and smile I answered "yes" but I really didn't understand what she meant by 'close' and I had never heard that expression used before then. Nonetheless, truly love them I did, and do.

Panicky present buying is never fun. Even worse when you're so broke you can't afford to pay attention. The cardigan, which beckoned me through the shop window, was the closest thing to a direct expression of love which I could fathom. It reminded me of one of those cream coloured V-neck jumpers which cricketers wear with white trousers on long summer evenings. They always look so athletic and important. The thought of wrapping my beloved Dad in a cream coloured V-neck cardigan, complete with furrowed cable stitch, two front pockets and leather football buttons was the closest representation of love that this awkward northern girl could muster. And so, with the last bit of money I had, I bought it for him. Leaving me too skint to buy my train ticket home.

Poor old Mum. What a rotten present she received from me that year. And the money to pay for it was borrowed at that. A homemade, fabric, hideous kind of jumper thing. It was far too huge for her tiny frame, truly vile and about as welcome as something the cat dragged in. We both knew it. I felt rotten. She deserved better. I had failed her. Resentment for my own short-sightedness, lack of funds and immaturity baked in deep.

Dad wore his cardy often. It fitted well and I loved seeing him in it. I'd like to think that this gift successfully conveyed something of the love I felt towards them both and was tangible evidence of my true feelings. A rare happy photograph of my smiling parents on holiday together in Malta shows Dad proudly wearing the cardigan, and my tough little Mum nestled up against him, her arms wrapped tightly around her husband and the cardigan I couldn't afford.

Many years later it somehow got passed back to me, and then to my daughter, who used it as a kind of slobbing around the house watching TV on cold days type of garment. Her adoring Grandad's Cardigan, though a little tattered by then, brought comfort. Somehow, without words, it shored up the link between her and the grandparents who sacrificed much to give her some measure of security.

3 Our Yarns

"Keep me as the apple of your eye; hide me in the shadow of your wings." Psalm 17:8 NIV.

Mother hen

Tiny flecks of thistle green and cornflower blue grow randomly across a woolly oatmeal landscape. Soft yellows spray sunny smudges sparingly atop broad high ridges. They cluster close, blown in and caught among the tracks laid down in precise parallel, along the linear valleys snaking in between. Grains of pink cling daringly to craggy folded escarpments. Paths worked deep weave their way by rounded broken-biscuit-hedgerows. They're drawn in tight to patchwork diamond fields of knits and pearls and basket weave. Rolling metal Caterpillar belts carve ribbed-stitched tractor marks, butt joined to eyelet-punctuated-fences, channelling downward to a winding coastal hem.

Forestation of the fabric spreads, gaining ground, as pills and bobbles spring up wild and rampant from too hot a wash and too mean a price. Belying power the sleeves fall plain and drab aside the drama of the body, whose turn-back-front folds open in a broad full-length lapel. It swings heavy, wide and free with each silent slippered movement.

Within this micro climate, a tiny holy island withstands the pounding storms and salted seas. Cascading over mossy heart beats, tender living tentacles of love grow care and peace. Each lives a while, then casts it seeds into that force-for-good which dwells outside of time. Until they rest and root with welcome on those with ears to hear and eyes to see.

Stillness of monastic depth waits gently, and without cost, for those who enter here, to breathe and be embraced and be. Until years three or four or five she fits well in here with me. Wrapped round with woolly wings of warmth she nestles close and rests. Curled up in the safety of that temporary regression her small frame falls limp and eyes quiet briefly in the black. Ten minutes tops. That's all and then the power nap is done.

Emerging bright with cheeks flushed red. Saucer eyes open to reveal our shared Forget-me-not-blue. Cast against her delicate porcelain-doll-features, contrasting thick dark hair is befitting of the noblest fairy tale heroine. A playful tickle to the tum and up she springs refreshed and calm. My good little bird, not an ounce of bother, recharged to cope with characteristic resilience for what remains of her water-splashing, letter-learning, playground-falling, chalk-brushed day.

Left behind, her baby soft breath blows through those waving yellow buttercups of joy. Pale fingerprints leave their silent touch of warmth in the softness of this mother land. Small five-toed-feet press seeds of love and calm into the rounded fleshy cup of my palm. Bliss leaks from my face. The willow of my heart lets down her un-cried tears of tension, soaking readily to quench my soul. And strands of blowing vine brush peace upon my arm. The warm milky scent of this mummy-cuddled-child lingers faintly on my speckled, scruffy cardigan.

And so I should, but cannot, wash it out.

The no-biscuit-biscuit blessing

Ancient fishermen fathers, water gypsies, mining disasters and the blackout. Snippets. Nothing more than that. Ancestral stories reliably slipped out, unannounced, over a cup of milky Methodist tea as weak as dishwater, alongside breaking news of Mrs Green's turfing failure. Some memories were slightly fluid and softly focussed, others pin sharp.

Rummaging for Kit Kats with my head cocooned in the fridge generated a fair bit of reverberation and I sometimes missed important details. The cunning mix of firm, cold chocolate and light, crisp wafer beckoned like an old friend. The beautiful memory of yesterday's mid-morning break fluttered around in my head like a trapped butterfly. My work day had been going badly and a raspy, tight chested panic squeezed my neck, the kind that ambushes lonely hearts, cruelly disabling them prior to a significant event.

I mentally flicked a shirty, irreverent, 999 call in the approximate direction of that which I perceive as God while the machine over filled a fragile plastic cup of equally plastic coffee. Thumb shoving coins into the second vending machine with force, I cynically made my demands. An urgent order for some indication of God's famous claim to be 'a very present help in times of trouble' was feebly placed. My muttering may have been audible as people were avoiding me. I determined to privately enjoy a master blend of sulky panic for the entire morning break. Some people just aren't happy if they're not miserable.

The snacks vending machine dispensed my Kit Kat. It was encased in a plastic foil wrapper instead of the original silver foil and paper sleeved wrapper. A disappointing marketing decision which denies many people of their familiar and well-loved ritual of creating a miniature silver 'brass rubbing' of the kit Kat logo. Their outrage has generated an online campaign. With 39 followers. I was tempted to make it 40. I concluded that everything was out of my control. That first bite surprised me. The second and third had me nodding silently with wide eyed approval as the party in my mouth kicked off. Like manna from heaven the vending machine had delivered a solid chocolate four finger Kit Kat entirely, yes entirely, devoid of wafer. Discovering that timely, no biscuit-biscuit blessing was legendary, as chocolate biscuit experiences go.

I emerged from the fridge into the kitchen where Dad's story telling continued. The pot dregs empty and yet I am home again. That kitchen. That place where love dwells. The door is not locked. The kettle is not cold. Neighbours and family come and go. Flanking Hydrangeas shift from playful pink to rich burgundy as summer unfolds into autumn. Exceedingly good cakes are kept in once expensive, yellowing not quite so-snappy Tupperware. A worn sticker on the teapot with rust brown innards still boasts of steel which is allegedly stainless. Its shallow spout dribbles impotently onto the Formica worktop. Glinting cars flick by. Fuchsia blooms pink and bright from Enid's hedge. Sally's horses run then nod pointlessly over the ill-placed gate of their long triangular field. The stories are told. And I really should have listened harder.

Stories were shared so frequently that their fabric lodged deep into the archive of my own memory and became an intrinsic part of me, whether I welcomed them or not. A bit of a clown at times some of Dad's tales were laugh out loud funny. But many were depressing stories of poverty, hardship, suffering and cold, which without exception ended in death. And on my day off, even with the kit Kat as a sweetener, I would really rather not have heard some of them.

Someone recently told me they choose not to look back over their shoulder into the past except to remind themselves of God's faithfulness to them. Is that what these stories were to my parents? Not perilous stories of defeat, under privilege, war and doom, but tangible reminders of survival, resourcefulness, hardiness, downright grit and divine blessing?

The legend of Sarah and Darius Taylor gripped me. As a descendant of the Taylors I always felt and understood the primal bent to sew and weave and clothe. It's about protection. This protectiveness dwells in each of us. We share it. And it binds our family together. Along with our toughness. Our resourcefulness. Our ever Northern-ness.

I press go and the archive of my mind plays the story once more:

Darius Taylor, possibly Dad's favourite ancestor, was mentioned often. He married Sarah. Their world seems far removed from my own and yet familiar. Sarah was a weaver and a knitter. Darius a fisherman, with the beating heart of a Tailor. Apparently, Sarah, praying in the oak pews of a Welsh chapel, was touched by inspiration.

I'm told that the footprint of many old churches forms the shape of a cross when seen from a bird's eye view. Later that day Sarah resumed work on the shawl she was currently knitting. As the days went by she crafted it into the shape of a cross leaving a long open slit along the nave, which is the lower part of the cross. The knitted sections parted just as the central aisle in a church parts the pews. Taking the widest part of the cross, the transept, she folded it over to join the edges. When the sides were stitched together they formed the seams of two sleeves and a bodice. By my Grandma's reckoning this was very possibly the first ever cardigan.

With the help of the minister's wife Sarah and Darius sent a sketch of her innovative yet unnamed design, by post, to Darius's Aunt Louisa, who was living in the north west of England. The letter was post marked 'Cardigan' and the name stuck. Dad chuckles: "And while the rest of the villagers were still flapping about in loose shawls, Sarah had fashioned a cardigan for Darius."

Sarah's letter did not survive the spoils of time. But the legend of Sarah and Darius Taylor, and the cardigan Sarah designed, endured as family folklore and was passed down to me. I'd like to say it was proudly passed down, but in reality it was spoken of quite incidentally, alongside bits of neighbourhood news, property maintenance issues and improbable ailments.

The whip hand

Monday morning diary time at my children's school was an exercise in storytelling of which I approved. Essentially the teacher instructed her pupils to write an account of personal events over their weekend. I often encouraged my children to reflect back on their experiences and verbally relay them to me in some detail, and so I readily bought into the Monday morning thing. Until I realised it could also be quite intrusive. And reveal things about family life which I would rather not be made public, thank you very much.

Money was seriously in short supply and so I became adept at making it stretch as far as possible. The Salvation Army Charity Shop became my friend. As I paid for my daughter's 'new' dress my happy little girl looked up and asked me: "What's this shop called Mummy?" I could see my darling child mentally formulating the Monday morning headlines of her diary. 'Mummy buys me second hand dress at Salvation Army Charity Shop' was not a story I could allow to leak into the public domain.

All too often I'd experienced the piercing sting of shame which poverty had so cruelly inflicted on my sensitive young life. My lazy materialistic reasoning regularly cast poverty and lack as the evil scientists who had surgically installed my every dysfunction. A deliberate, self-serving, game of blame which successfully exonerated me from any personal responsibility for my own failings for decades. It was just easier that way.

Fierce protectiveness generated a driving need to spare my children from being inflicted with those same wounds, or any wounds. So I quickly answered my daughter's question with a nod and a wink to the assistant: "Debenhams darling, this shop is called Debenhams." An outright lie, which I'm not proud to admit, but hardly regret.

Seven years later, armed with some gift vouchers and well substantiated rumours of a genuine fifty per cent off sale; I bravely entered those hallowed halls of consumerism and made my first ever bona fide Debenhams purchase. This was shopping for new things. Things which had never been owned by anyone else. Proper shopping. In a proper shop. Like proper people do. Nay, this was proper shopping in a real life, fancy pants, high street Department Store. The giddy girl in my head squealed: "Look at me now! I'm shopping in the real Debenhams!"

Two cardigans. Yes, two!

One a deep ribbed, dark earthy green with broad roped cable stitched cuffs and a generous shawl collar, long and button-less with a tie belt. I've boasted of its enduring style and faultless brand name quality to any who will listen, but the truth is I've worn it little, and washed it even less. It falls open in an unflattering robe like fashion and in any case I must preserve it to remember my moment of unquestionable transcendence from upper working class to lower middle class which it so obviously represents, in the way only a Debenhams cardigan can.

The second cardigan is a shorter, helpfully zipped style, with a generous hood, classic stone beige and

100% cotton. Six rows of cable stitch furrow the front, and deep cuffs at the wrists and waist give it a pleasing structure and a country pub wear-ability. I must have washed it wrong 'cos it's become quite stiff to the touch, the sleeves have become narrow and too tight to squeeze a tissue in, and the hood falls awkwardly on my shoulders, intrusively jockeying for position with my hair, but it's a fab cardy, nonetheless.

My Debenhams cardys impress me far more than they really deserve to. True, they are well made, and quality does matter to me. But they also symbolize my realization of independence; the secure feeling that the ability to pay bills on time brings; filling the boot of the car with shopping bags of food for yet another week; not being beholden to someone else for the roof over my children's head; changing a light bulb; being called a name other than Mum, and knowing that someone will pay me money for a job of work. They are tangible evidence of that tiny imperceptible upwards shift on the personal and social strata, heralding in some measure of stability and a more financially secure life for my family.

4 Their Yarns

"Put that on your needles and knit it." Grandma Kitty

Breakdown in communications

Tina spent two hours pampering and preening while George sat contentedly before the TV watching the rugby match he had automatically recorded on the black box. She had mentally chosen her party dress three days earlier on the packed train home from work while standing squashed between a sulky head-phoned teenager and a tall sweaty man whose buttocks pressed into the small of her back every time the train stopped. The sudden jet of warm air slowly rising up her spine, she convinced herself, was not his fart. Absolutely not.

Accessories were mentally selected earlier this morning when she was busily scrubbing the black mould and orange slime from deep inside her mother's fridge while simultaneously trying not to gag.

Her doubts about the fit of the dress evaporated as the discreet side zip slid effortlessly up over her hips and waist with a satisfyingly glide. Tina was excited to be going out in the evening for the first time in a long time. Sipping a glass of red and belting out 'Feel Like a Woman' with Shania Twain she had a little spin around the bedroom. Sliding her painted toe nails into a pair of three and a half inch heels, she finally made her appearance to George.

"All ready then?" she asked him casually, while secretly hoping for some kind of a compliment. "Huh, you'll freeze like that love, especially when the riverboat gets moving, haven't you got a woolly cardigan?"

"Boat! What boat? You never said anything about a boat!"

Chemical or otherwise

Rosa's fingertips explored each panel. Leaning in closely her eyes examined the tightness and uniformity of each stitch. Basket weave, purl, eyelets and lace, cables and twist, deep grids and honeycombs. Then she stepped back to survey the creative whole. The white brick wall behind, was a washed out foil for the striking blend of colours which neither matched nor jarred. Three metres by two in all, Rosa pictured the patchwork blanket draped heavily over an impressive king size bed; she pictured the bedroom, then the home, then the wedding.

"There are five buttons left and I will need six please Rosa" came the interruption to her day dream. The customer was a Saturday morning regular, who met with a group of ladies in the adjoining coffee shop each week. The little group would knit and chat together for hours while others came and went after stocking up with patterns, needles and yarn. If the shop wasn't busy, sometimes she would sit with them, her fingers working on the frothy silk ruffles of a cardigan she was making to wear over a sleeveless bridesmaid dress. She had made that too.

As a young girl travelling abroad with her Dad she had seen for herself the horrors of the sweat shops. Looking into the gaunt faces of children her own age slaving for a pittance, she staunchly refused to buy or wear anything without a full understanding of its provenance. A line of thinking which would eventually birth her ethical baby, the Yarn Barn.

Located in the yard of her Grandparent's Lancashire farm, Rosa had originally commandeered a corner of the old barn for a summer spinning and knitting group. Today it was a booming enterprise, modern aisles of wool and patterns were peopled by half manikins clothed in cosy hand knitted gorgeousness. Rosa's favourites were the cloth covered toddlers, a faceless boy and girl, whom she would dress in little cardigans, hats and scarfs which she had knitted. She had fun adding buttons from the vast range in store, some shaped like cute little owls, pencils and trucks.

At just 35, she was considered to be a successful business woman, with a renowned integrity regarding the textile industries, stocking her shelves with only the most ethically produced materials. Among customers she was known, not only as a trusted friend, but also as an expert needlewoman tackling innovative projects many wouldn't attempt, as evidenced by the long waiting list for her evening workshops.

After twenty years of following knitting patterns created by others, Rosa finally felt confident enough to design her own hand knitted range; one which she hoped might express her ideas and provide a platform to highlight awareness of exploitation in the textile industry, an injustice which had long troubled her. Negotiations with the pattern book publishers were all lined up.

Dropping her off at the train station Alan reassured her with a genuine conviction about her ability: "You'll be fine doll; they gonna love your ideas; I've seen you get where water can't; this is going to happen for you!"

She kissed him and smiled: "Thanks, it's just that I've been my own boss for so long now, meeting sponsors scares me stiff, so I've asked the group to pray for me."

Alan laughed roguishly his deep brown eyes narrowing cheekily: "You're mental! I still can't understand why someone with your brains would buy into all that hocus pocus!"

"Don't be like that" she purred "you know it's helped me before."

"Correlation doesn't equal causality" he announced proudly as if he were the originator of the quote.

Rosa hopped out of the car, slinging one strap over her head she draped the bag across her body and grabbed a large portfolio from the back seat. Fully focussed on presenting her designs to the sponsors, she knew this was not the best moment for a debate with Alan about abstract, unproven concepts. She hopped on the Pendalino and settled down to review her presentation.

"Listen mate, I'm telling you straight up, attraction is based purely on the need to reproduce, and love is just a brain chemical to ensure the survival of the species, that's why women get frisky when they're ovulating! Keep it in perspective, there's plenty more fish in the sea." Alan ended his macho little speech by sitting up straighter in the faux leather pub chair, a satisfied grin merged slyly upwards into a knowing nod aimed in Grant's direction. Grant's eyes focussed beyond Alan, on the slim figure of a woman behind him, his mouth unconsciously mee mawed a silent warning before shaping awkwardly into a toothy smile: "Rosa! You're back early!"

"A brain chemical? That's what love is to you? Is that what we have?" she spat, dropping her bag to the ground and waving one arm at him in a subconscious slap. Alan spluttered a string of excuses about not knowing she was behind him, about how he was trying to comfort their friend who'd been dumped, about blokey banter not being meant for a woman's ears, until finally asserting: "Listen babe, all this mumbo jumbo you believe in about true love and hope and romance and prayers and God, it's too airy fairy for me, until something has been proven scientifically I can't believe it! I'm not going to believe it, because it just can't be true until it's proven and nothing else makes sense. You can't prove any of the faith stuff you believe, it's all bollocks, you can't even prove the existence of God."

"And you can't disprove it" Rosa shot back at him before striding defiantly towards the exit. She didn't look back, not even to check if she had gathered up all her stuff.

In class, a normally bouncy Alan struggled to focus; two of his pupils picked up on this and spied their chance to mess about with the Bunsen burner. Flopping into an empty chair next to them he implored weakly: "C'mon lads, give the old man a break will ya? I've had a rough weekend." They looked at each other sceptically, and to Alan's surprise, switched off the Bunsen burner and asked "What's up sir?" He didn't respond, just ground his way dutifully through the lesson, Rosa's parting words still playing in his mind.

"Can we talk?" Alan nervously texted "OK" came her reply.

The old canal path was popular with dog walkers and cyclists, an occasional barge would chug slowly by, its occupants nodding politely to the land lubbers. Alan and Rosa walked less than a metre apart, hands stuffed in pockets.

"It can't end like this Rosa, I care for you, I'm sorry if the things I said hurt you, but I meant them, that's just who I am, you have to accept that." Alan said softly, his hand lightly touching her arm.

"I care for you too Alan, I thought I loved you, I thought you might even be the one. I get your assertions about science I really do, I want to understand things through my intellect as well. But what I'm about is more than that. There are other parts of me, other channels through which I understand and read the world around me. I can't prove those channels exist, I just know they are there, I know there is more than chemicals and facts and I won't let my life be constrained by that way of thinking, it would suffocate me! Just 'cos something isn't proven doesn't mean it doesn't exist for me, I'm ok with not knowing everything for certain, with some mystery, some unknowns."

Turning squarely towards her Alan took her hand in his: "I love you Rosa, chemical or otherwise, and I want to be with you." He pulled her closer: "Did those London guys agree to sponsor your designs?"

Leaning against him she looked up and grinned lob sidedly: "Yip, and you had faith in that idea long before it was a proven fact didn't you?!"

5 Under the Sun

"There is a time to plant and a time to uproot." Ecclesiastes 3:2 NIV.

Season of the fallow soul

If you didn't know it was there, you wouldn't have known it was there. It was that kind of a place. Secretly tucked away at the end of a narrow, dusty farm track which seemed to be going nowhere. Unruly hawthorns spilled over unchecked and little sparrows flitted about near the ground in a friendly, welcoming, no-cats-around-here sort of way. Entering in through the heavy creak of age old doors, the more than a metre thick walls immediately imposed their protective, palpably parental embrace.

The tiny isolated chapel was gloriously saturated by centuries of extravagant prayer and worship which seeped into the ether as earthy living breath, its peppery scent caressing everything it touched. A dissonant blend of gentleness and strength infused this holy of holies gateway, hidden away deep in the heart of Englandshire.

The building had been decommissioned and transformed into a stylish office which was home to a successful private company. Circumstances beyond my control meant I was the family breadwinner, and with school age children to feed and a mortgage to pay, I was reluctantly there out of grim necessity to do a most unglamorous, ordinary job of work for them.

On arrival I quickly began to feel like a fly on the wall of a Hugh Grant film set. Or at least a voyeur working behind the scenes as this private middle class reality show was being filmed. I observed up close the thoroughly posh, yet astonishingly unspoiled and likeable, team at work and play. This remarkable, tiny band of kind, well educated men were never shouty or aggressive. They knew how to do everything well. How to dress well, run meetings well, resolve problems well and most importantly how to say no well.

Even inside the walls of this, their own personal fiefdom, safely hidden from the view of friends and enemies alike, they were respectful towards each other. Clients, and women in particular, were welcomed with a wonderfully effortless, silky charm which was as delectable to behold as it was to be the subject of. My employers were perfect gentlemen who graciously forgave my blunders. I grew to trust them, to feel safe again, and the chapel smiled approvingly.

But entering this season was tough. It demolished the hopes of my aspiring ego which crashed down like the Berlin wall, drawing into the open that taunting I-told-you-so mind mob. My struggle was worsened because I was too short sighted to recognise this season for what it was. Following a turbulence which rendered me not fit for dog meat I jibbed against the change because, for all the world, it looked like certain failure. I'd bombed. A backwards step as dead end and insignificant as the iffy dirt track I had dubiously followed to get there.

A wise and trusted friend so clearly saw what I could not: "Don't be in a hurry to leave this season of rest which God has provided for you. Be patient." With characteristically prideful resistance, cunningly passed off as glowing ambition, I endeavoured to leave those annoyingly twee words behind in the place they had been spoken. But they would not leave me. Every day they followed me all the way to work like that little lamb of Mary's. Surrounded by fertile farmland, once stale book learning about crop rotation now sprung to life in my mind. I saw with my own eyes how the real life farmer, reassuringly wellied and flat-capped, ploughed and tilled the land to eradicate weeds but allowed some fields to lie fallow, un-seeded, for one or more growing seasons to regain fertility for the next crop. In farming, that's just how it is.

The work itself was fairly undemanding and repetitive. Freed from the heavy responsibilities of being a key player I was surprised by how much I was able to take in from my ringside seat. Gleaning tips about running a business in a commercially viable way became a regular, though unconscious activity. I learned how to operate efficient systems and run methodical processes. I observed calm, courteous professionalism executed under pressure during most shifts.

I noted how client's accounts were proactively managed with drive and passion. It was like the old saying about when the student is ready the teacher will arrive. Nutrient rich rain quenched the parched bare earth of my fallow soul. Repair and growth were happening at a deep cellular level, and when I wasn't obsessively grumping about my rubbish lot in life, I occasionally remembered how to smile.

A fully paid up invitation to the Office Christmas 'do' in Barcelona was an extravagant treat which, oiled by the aforementioned effortless silky charm, I was easily persuaded to accept. Most Christmas do's I'd attended consisted of a Christmas Eve pie and a pint in the pub over the road. The toffs, however, worked hard and played hard. The brief flight arrived at midday and we were soon navigating the beautiful streets of Barcelona.

The detailed architecture was stunning and the city had a decadent cultural feel to it. We trogged around for hours occasionally pit-stopping in and out of cafes. In spite of a poor choice in heels, the onset of a slightly dodgy knee, and carrying the weight of excess timber on my backside, I climbed most of the way up the Gaudi 'Cathedral' to be proudly rewarded by spectacular views over the city.

It was December and as the late afternoon temperatures began to dip I was obviously chilled. Without hesitation one of my bosses escorted me into a fancy boutique. Once inside, against my resistance, he insisted on buying a beautiful hand knitted cardigan for me. I was stunned by his kindness and chivalry. The cool evening fell; the new cardigan kept me wonderfully snug, and as our little band of Brits roamed the Spanish city I was able to fully enjoy the lively buzz of local bars and taverns. My Barcelona cardigan still speaks to me of that spell of kindness, rest and recovery, and how an uninvited season of the fallow soul prepared the ground for a wholly unanticipated harvest.

June

A piercing, thorny jab punctured the soft pink flesh with biting sharpness. The first stab was quickly followed by another, then another, completing a neat row of six bloody holes. Treddling along an invisible path, the offending wounds were inflicted with the speed of an expert seamstress on *piece work, the pointed tip of her steel needle disappearing into the defenceless fabric of my flesh at equal intervals. The angry fizzing wasp would have scurried on to circumnavigate my entire abdomen in a blind, stinging frenzy had I not reluctantly reached my hand in to quickly scoop it out of my pants. With all the grace of a beer soaked Morris dancer I flung him down onto our garden path, squealed like a pig, and stomped out my defiant dance of the dominant species, until the knicker infiltrator fizzed no more.

Geneva was hot in June. Considered pre-holiday cardigan shopping was required. Where would I find my essential travel kit? Where could I purchase the very lightest of summer cardigans? Something un-squashable. Which wouldn't wrinkle in the only piece of hand luggage I was planning to take. Something casual enough for long morning strolls, light enough to protect delicate bare shoulders from the baking heat of the day, heavy enough to afford warmth on a chilly night, rugged enough to be tied around the waist or firmly looped onto the strap of a handbag. Something classy enough to be casually arranged over shoulders for evenings dining out in this most sophisticated of European cities. Where could I shop for this answer to everything cardigan? Selfridges? John Lewis? Next? Naah, Matalan was the cheapest.

The famous fountain plume was spectacular, this blessed place of peace making a cosmopolitan delight. High above the city an early morning walk took us through rolling meadows sprinkled red with field poppies. An ascending dusty path came to rest at a huge wizened oak tree, the wide span of its leafy branches casting a circle of shaded, bare earth. The parched timber bench, which appeared to have grown up through the ground at the base of the trunk, was perfectly positioned to take in long views of the deep green valley stretching out to the horizon before us.

Lake Geneva glinted postcard perfect in the distance. Swiss chalets nestled in the hillside of a sunny Switzerland I didn't expect, their snow-less roofs and open shutters quite unlike the blue-shadowed painting by numbers image of a Christmas past. A vast cloudless sky hovered breathlessly above the oak, splashing warm sunlight down onto our faces through the colander of back-lit emerald leaves. Laying my Geneva cardigan along the bench for protection the rough woody fibres snagged readily against the thin brown jersey, inadvertently confirming the poor quality of the fabric and the cheapness of the wearer. We sat down upon it nonetheless, the broad girth of the trunk providing a welcome lean. Close against each other, yet far away from our every day cares, the hot foreign breeze kissed away our tension. We began reflecting upon our blessings with that authentic ascending gratefulness of the heart which some call prayer.

BUZZZZZZ! BUZZZZZ! I leapt to my feet in a flash! Hopping and screaming I repeatedly slapped the place where the loud buzzing sound was emanating from inside my pants. Determined not to be the victim of multiple belly stings again, I belted that brazen trespasser with such vigour the buzzing eventually stopped and, apart from my half bent over wheezing gasps and seasonal country sounds, the air fell silent once again. Braced for the task of removing the offending critter, whose goopy innards were most likely flattened to my flesh, I squeamishly armed myself with a tissue. A tentative search about my person revealed that the mobile phone in my pocket, set to a buzzing vibration when a message came in, had just about survived the bashing.

*piece work – workers paid per piece of work they complete

I kill butterflies

I kill butterflies. Occasionally bees. Sometimes wasps. Frequently flies. Every day. They die in the intense heat of our glass conservatory. It troubles me.

Hot spells send me ferreting for winter coats and extra thick woollies. That's the optimum time to give them a wash because they aren't needed and will dry quickly. The washing line was filling up nicely. Coats hung heavily from their hangers, crumpled fabric threatening their ruin. Squeezing soggy knitwear in the sink tired my swollen hands. The dash outside to slosh wares over the line delivered a welcome spray of water to a body blushed with heat. Wooden pegs clipped washing to the plastic coated line.

Three cardigans hung in a row, arms pegged wide to keep the shape. Bleeding water to the ground they drew darkness on the paving below. Following the lie of the land drips wiggled their way, each following the one before it, processing downwards in a channel before diving under the paving stones. Stooping to retrieve a peg the cardigans silhouetted themselves against the sun, forcing an uncomfortable reminder of that scene in history when three men were hung out to dry. I watched for a second but had to turn away.

The conny is a floor hopping 33° Celsius. 50 flies buzz around in the apex of the glass roof, 67 lie dead. Two wasps and two butterflies lie motionless on the hot tiles. Nine delicate butterflies still cling to life here and there. How I long to rescue them.

I've taken five outside, four flew away, one sits motionless. It remains upright, wings closed vertically. "Just fly outside" I mutter to the remaining captives pointing in an exaggerated fashion at the open doors. Filthy flies surge and drone in the glass apex. A longing to lift the lid off this giant jam jar creeps over me.

Butterflies should live in my garden not my home, colourfully feeding on the patio flowers while bringing me delight. Is that too much to ask? Retreating to the kitchen I sulk and make a pot of Kenyan coffee, a substance not known for calming people down, cooling people off, or helping stranded butterflies.

Now there are six butterflies in the conservatory, two dead ones remain dead and the rescued one on the patio does not look well. All are innocent players in this private suburban drama in which I am cast as the Angel of Death.

Every door and window has been wide open for over three hours and yet all the butterflies remain stubbornly huddled together in the same dead end corner. Disproportionate sadness dulls the bright blue behind the mashed potato clouds. Powerlessness pales the swishing leafy greens. Immobilisation crawls over me like a swarm of black ants and I feel that suffocating, twitchy, shallow-breathed, frozen brand of panic.

The pain my husband and I felt when we lost our parents one by one returns. Out of nowhere grief encircles me, closing in to ambush my battered heart. I share in the grief a family member has plunged into as his sister, a young woman in her thirties, died just two days ago, leaving a son aged fourteen without a mum.

Like a cavalry on the horizon a vicar's story gallops to my mind. While out for a walk by the sea the vicar spotted a sheep trapped and bleating on a cliff-side ledge. Alarmed by this he informed the local farmer, who was very grateful. Four days later the vicar saw the sheep was still trapped on the ledge. He immediately went to visit the farmer and challenged him. The old farmer explained that he had to wait until the frightened sheep was so weak it wouldn't have the strength to object to the rescue. Experience had taught him that if he climbed down the steep cliff face to rescue the sheep too soon she would struggle, panic, kick and put them both in danger of falling during the treacherous climb to safety.

With this principle in mind I close the doors and windows. When the butterflies are stilled and weakened by the heat I will tease them onto a piece of paper and release them. Twenty minutes pass and they become subdued. In my hunt for a sheet of paper I find the list of things which I should be doing today. Rescuing butterflies is not on it. An eye-rolling reprimand is given and ignored. Two brown butterflies slide readily onto the paper and fly away when released.

But the Whites won't co-operate. Each approach sends them higher into the heat and certain death. The sun has burned some clouds away and the south-westerly, glass roofed conservatory takes the full hit of direct heat. Thirty minutes of teetering around precariously at the top of a ladder, sweat dripping unattractively down my face, squadrons of flies dive bombing my head in an alarmingly organised fashion, and I fold. Some saviour I am.

I google for clues. Indications are that butterflies actually like warm conservatories. This doesn't help me. I wave my arms around. I flick water near them. I shout at them. "Leave now or you will die!" I worry what my neighbours must think. I worry I haven't done a single task on today's agenda. Dead flies rain to the floor. The rescued butterfly on the patio flops over. And my heart whispers that this whole drama is really about my need to rescue, to save, to act out a mission that doesn't end in loss, death and disappointment but ends instead with life and liberty. To be rightfully re-cast as a deliverer not an Angel of Death.

More realisations quickly follow. I realise that I've done my level best to help them and I can't help them anymore, that nature does its own thing and death is a part of that. And so I think "OK, have it your way". In resignation I open the doors, place a damp sponge near the remaining sleepy butterflies, say a prayer, leave them to make their own choice and begin researching mesh screens.

6 Meetings

"Even a slug leaves a silver trail" Val Fraser

Where everybody knows your name

'I'm here' reads the incoming text. I turn off the torch and abort my efforts to insert those fiddly 'Party Feet' gel insoles into the darkness of my new boots. The insoles aren't remotely sticky. And there's no diagram with the instructions which appear to have been written by a cave man. It's an operation not dissimilar to inserting a raw egg back into its shell. For the eighth time I think I've secured them in place. With a victorious sigh I slide my foot into the boot. The insole seems to jump playfully aside, laughing "missed me!" and I wonder if that's why they're called Party Feet. I mumble something unladylike, quickly zip up my boots, grab a coat, jump in the car and zoom off to where I should already be.

The waitress is a family friend and always remembers what I have to drink. She should, I've had enough coffee in here to qualify as a shareholder. She's already written my order down and is genuinely surprised when I decide to forgo my usual drug of choice and try a milder option. We share a laugh and have a quick chat as she prepares my brew. It gives me a good feeling to be 'Where everybody knows my name'. Those lyrics from the theme tune of American sitcom 'Cheers' used to ring out every Friday back in the nineties . . . or was it the eighties?

When I think about it properly I realise everybody in here doesn't actually know my name at all. Just this one waitress knows my name. But I like her a lot and she's always genuinely cheerful and pleased to see me, she always asks after my family members by name and so I feel made welcome. I find myself marvelling at the difference just one person has made to my overall experience.

As I'm paying I notice another waitress leave her post behind the counter. She makes her way over to a white haired lady who is sitting alone. I'll call her Mildred. Her cup and saucer are placed centrally upon an empty dinner plate. Next the cutlery is aligned neatly upon it. Methodically swiping up imaginary crumbs from the table with her napkin and dropping them into the cup, Mildred then folds and tucks it securely under the saucer, ready for an easy one handed removal of the entire pile.

On the chair next to Mildred sits a large bag which is somewhere between a shopping bag and a handbag, the straps arch in parallel like a double rainbow waiting to be picked up by the hand of God. Draped over the back of the chair is a blue green cardigan which perfectly matches the short sleeved jumper she is wearing. The bag and cardigan wait in obedient silence for their master to arise. Two limbless tubular sleeves fall in a stiff downwards arrangement towards the worn lino of the chessboard floor. Like a child's arms they reach expectantly down into the earth hoping to summon up the embrace of a long dead parent but none is forthcoming. An army of hand knitted stitches, united in their symmetrically chevroned ranks, march in empty protest against the thieving, silent grave.

As the waitress approaches Mildred's face lifts into a familiar friendly smile. They have a little chat and exchange the briefest touch of a hand. Taking the blue green cardigan from the back of the chair the waitress positions herself behind Mildred and begins the process of gently jiggling the cardigan up her arms, first one then the other. For a few seconds her own arms reach around to the front of Mildred encircling her in a faux embrace. As the cardigan is placed over welcoming shoulders the brief operation is completed and the pearl-less partners of the hand stitched twin set are reunited.

And I smile.

Yet I'm simultaneously envious. That moment of simple human contact seems so meaningful. I seriously consider the idea of becoming a waitress. Much like a kindly nurse, minus the scary diseases and disgusting body fluids. An angel dispensing coffee and cake of above average quality. Bestowing smiles and warmth to the lost and the lonely, while radiating an inexplicable glow.

But then I remember the wholly wretched, ungracious individual that I am, with barely a shred of patience for the down trodden. Or the slightly smelly. Or the odd. Or even the shabbily dressed. And I have an obsessive need to clean up crumbs and mess. And I repeatedly disinfect every surface that has ever been touched by human hand. And I have a nose big enough to smell bacteria from ten feet away, even when I do have a stinking cold. And when I drink coffee I can talk a glass eye to sleep.

I reconsider the waitress idea. I opt instead to put £3.50 into the Salvation Army bucket being held by a pleasant young man. They do a marvellous job of caring for the down trodden and radiating an inexplicable glow. And it was, I am reliably informed, a Sally Army Officer who made egg and chips for my Dad while he was serving in North Africa, just after the war, bringing comfort and joy and briefly making him feel closer to home. And I marvel again at the difference just one person can make to an overall experience.

Longing to Belong

"I do apologise, I'm afraid we're running late" she smiled. I'm directed to a cosy seating area and asked to wait. There's a great buzz about this place and I greedily drink it in. It's a far cry from the isolation of my home office and the main reason I recklessly applied for a job here. I've often met my sister for a coffee in the public Bistro of this plush ten million pound retirement village, so it feels very familiar.

With a totally irrelevant background in writing and communications I was astonished, yet excited, to get an interview for a receptionist position. Fantasies about all the lovely people I will meet, the community connections, the fun works' outings, the team spirit, the inspiring residents, the free gym membership, the weight loss and the extra spending money are awakened.

During my half hour wait I chat with three delightfully cheerful residents. I want to scoop them up and take them home. Having recently lost both my parents, following twenty years of heavy involvement in their lives, I'm really missing caring for people. This feels like a good place to give and receive some warmth and in the friendly atmosphere I feel momentarily relaxed.

The window cill is home to a Lead Crystal vase of beautiful snow white Lilies. What a lovely human touch. The water is almost gone and I wonder if I should top it up. A closer inspection reveals no scent, the Lilies are fake and so is the water in the vase. Which I cynically concede is not Crystal. But I just can't bear to touch it and learn the truth.

Leaning into the trendy but uncomfortable purple sofa I sit upright trying to project cleverness and efficiency. Pulling nervously at the single button of a too tight cardigan cutting into my middle I wrestle with questions about moving forwards or moving backwards. I wonder if, like in the cardigan, my wrongly shaped bits will feel trapped.

"This way please." Beyond the plush reception lounge a coded door reveals a surprisingly colourless carpet-less stairwell. I ascend far too noisily. At last I'll meet my new team mates, my fellow party-goers, and fulfillers of all my needs! How excited they must be.

My smart outfit feels too 'try-hard'. The interviewers are dressed down. Right down. I mean like they've slept at the office all week kind of down. "You're application states you're not available on Sundays and I need full flexibility" cuts the opening line. Whaaat?

"You must work every other Sunday morning." Then why oh why have I been selected for interview? I interpret this bark as: "I'm running thirty mintes behind, skipping this interview will get things back on track."

There's no warm welcome, jokey introductions, inappropriate prying or clumsy attempt to put me at ease. The anticipated neutral small talk about weather, travel and parking perfected by HR types is not on the agenda. I'm momentarily rattled and the fake Lilies remind me of my hopefully naive projections.

The opening statements, formal gathering of signatures and lengthy scenario questions are strictly adhered to. They play by the book, move quickly along, leaving no room for inconsequential chat, charm, soft or hard sell, name dropping, blackmail, blather or blag. The questions are tick-box procedural, unrelenting, and tough. I decide to stay calm, think on my feet and answer as best I can.

Two scenarios refer to the handling of confidential documents and phone calls while on the reception desk, which is located in a public space, twenty paces (I measured) from a main road. My examiners assert that the onus falls on me to maintain confidentiality and want a clear explanation of how exactly I'll achieve this. "By sitting somewhere else" is not the required answer. I bluster something about locking documents in drawers and speaking quietly on the phone.

This non-negotiable verbal test isn't a mutual getting to know each other. The whole deal is on their terms. There will be no concessions for my requirements. I pity the desperate, jobless soul playing this high stakes game. I start to feel like a silly, selfish, fraud for applying for a job which I don't really need.

My interrogators splutter a weary laugh when I play the clown. They show polite interest in my answers and fervently scribble notes and scores as if their very lives depend upon it. And I glance into their eyes for a fleeting second and see the heavy burden that they carry. They aren't looking for a new pal, an office joker, or a good laugh at the works 'do'. They are the guardians of elderly, vulnerable adults, a good number of whom are really quite seriously ill and in need of round the clock care.

The final question addresses procedures surrounding allegations of abuse. A cool social temperature suddenly plummets below zero. This dark freezing chill forces an emotional shudder down each spine. What I initially perceive as a prickly attitude towards me I now interpret as fierce protection of the people entrusted to their care. And it slowly dawns on me that I'm standing at the access point to those dear folk. This is the way in. Those people, who like my own beloved parents, having lived their lives, now seek peace and safety within these walls. The decision that these gatekeepers make today, I realise, must be backed up by concrete evidence, strict procedures and sound judgement. This is serious business and they certainly treat it as such. And as miffed as I am to be grilled rather than greeted I take it on the chin in light of the fearsome weight of responsibility which they carry.

Coat off. Kettle on. Phone rings. I'm invited for a second interview. Will I be attending? You bet I will. On second thoughts. Naah.

Terry the tie

Tomato soup. Or possibly ketchup. One of those two anyway. The dried out tear drop shape grew thicker towards its lower edge, forming a firm plasticy up-curled rim standing about 2mm proud of his chequered tie. I was immediately reminded of a baby's catch all bib. Which, I reasoned, this chap should probably have worn.

Terry-the-tie sheepishly slid the third bundle of papers across the desk towards me. Eyes blinking in quick succession as he lowered his gaze. He knew he was pushing his luck, but maybe he needed the commission so badly that he decided to chance his arm. "Ok so now you've seen our higher risk investment packages, our lower risk packages offer a slightly different approach. I'll just run quickly through them with you, is that alright?" I nodded in polite resignation, my brain a mush of figures, percentages and estimated returns. Terry trotted out his script while turning the pages. His faith in my ability and willingness to understand him appeared to be slipping. All the while I was questioning if I had reached saturation point and couldn't actually retain any more facts. And even if I could, did I really want to?

Questions about the wisdom of taking important advice from a financial 'expert' who lacked the focus, concentration and hand eye coordination to accurately insert food into his own mouth began to formulate in my mind. Was I willing to trust such a person? Could I hand over precious once-in-a-lifetime inherited money to someone who had either a) left the house without checking his appearance? Or b) had such poor powers of observation that he hadn't noticed the red stain on his chequered tie? Or (c) . . . a harsh judgemental list of questions tumbled rapidly into my head, accompanied by a cruel caustic wit which did not cast Terry-the-Tie in a favourable light.

Admittedly, the splodgy stain hadn't entirely taken me by surprise. I'd been forewarned. A relative was also bequeathed an inheritance, also banked here, also had a phone call and subsequent meeting with good old Terry. She also became transfixed by the soup/ketchup splodge/stain, and subsequently she also declined his advice. In spite of the warning I decided to give Terry the benefit of the doubt and attend the meeting. "So what do you think Mrs Fraser? Are you a high, low or medium risk taker?"

Latino loops chivvied up noisily from deep inside the chunky ribbed knit stitching of my third best cardigan pocket. Piercing the corporate starkness of this meeting room down in the bowels of the bank with an inappropriate, impossible to ignore, bouncy little ring. "I'm so sorry, I'll have to take that." I reached into my pocket, flipped open my phone, the incoming text message from a relative read: "Is the stain still there?"

Supressing an involuntary snort, I scraped back the chair and said sheepishly: "Thanks so much, got to dash, I'll have to think about it."

7 Mums and Nurses

"You knit me together in my mother's womb." Psalm 139:13 NIV.

Holding my own

Skipping lightly up the steps of the dog leg staircase, my normally worn out Mum, suddenly took on the girlish mannerisms of an excited teenager. Bouncing onto the half way landing she stopped. Spinning around on her toes to face me, she displayed an energy and lightness of spirit which I hadn't seen since my Dad playfully wolf whistled at her, some ten years earlier. A pleasant smile lifted her tired face and for a second her part sunken eyes were elevated to that former striking emerald green.

It was 30°c. Mum's baby pink imitation cashmere cardigan was still redundantly flopped over the wrought iron banister rail where it had been placed on the first day of her arrival. The tiny bead-like buttons drooped sadly downwards in their continued estrangement from the button holes which were made for them. The machine stitched slits remained closed, their unperceivable openings barely able to accommodate even those smallest of buttons without a forceful shove of the thumb.

The new dress, a rich chocolate brown, was synched in at her impressively small waist. This was her first shopping trip to Dallas, Texas. The exclusive department store, Neiman Marcus, located in downtown Dallas, provided Mum with an exciting, confidence boosting experience. A slim English woman in Texas was doubly rare, and the commission based sales assistant made a big fuss of her. And the dress, that simple, elegant dress brought her to life in a way I never knew a dress could.

And that's when it happened. She spoke those words. In that way. Dispensing what was to be her first and only piece of wisdom in regard to a woman's appearance. I can't recall us ever having any 'girly' conversations about makeup, perfume, hair or clothes. We never went shopping or did Mother-daughter things together and so for me, this was huge. The sum total of her knowledge in that area was being passed down from her generation to mine. And I almost missed it.

Transfixed by her sudden personality change, I was distracted from receiving her message. She looked really good, she seemed to feel good too. Her tiny frame was elevated about six feet above my own as I stood at the foot of the staircase. The half way landing briefly became her own personal stage, generously lending its authority and drama to her neat little figure. Mum was shorter than me. But in the act of looking up at her I became her child again, triggering a conditioned response within me. Now I felt compelled to pay attention and listen really hard. I'm so glad I did. As I write I can see her in my mind's eye. Once again I press the play button:

In mock preening she smoothed the soft fabric of the dress down, gliding both hands over her slender hips with a glance of satisfied approval. She was smiling so hard her whole face was lifted and for a second, I thought she might actually break into a laugh. Looking straight at me she triumphantly announced: "I don't have to be the

Belle of the ball (pause for effect) but I do like to hold my own." Exit stage right.

I got the feeling she loved that dress! More significantly I think she loved herself in it. At least in that moment, she was confident, unshakable. She didn't ask for my opinion or hang around for my response. She just made her declaration and split. She wasn't fishing for compliments. She clearly didn't want mine, or anyone else's opinion regarding the dress, or her in it, for that matter.

Mum's words, and the surprising mini performance with which they were delivered, have long stayed with me. I've often unpicked that eighteen-word-fifteen-second scene in the midnight hours when I'm trying to figure out what it means to be a woman. Unravelling their meaning, their delivery, their significance. Replaying the fading, grainy video tape that lives in my head, trying to tune in better, turn up the volume, zoom in and pause her exit long enough to ask a question. Longing to revisit that moment and extract a mysterious something from it. Mum "couldn't abide" long sermons. "If they can't make their point in fifteen minutes they shouldn't be ministers" she'd say. She managed to make her point in just 15 seconds.

The women closest to me have heard me say: "My Mum used to say 'I don't have to be the belle of ball, but I do like to hold my own.' " Truth is, she said it just that once, but I've replayed it many times. How should I be as a woman? The answer was there all the time, much like those which are cleverly hidden within an exam paper, if you're canny enough to search for them.

It seems to me that 'Holding My Own' is simply about being satisfied with my own appearance and, don't miss this now, the amount of effort I have put into achieving it. It's a state of mind which is totally disconnected from any frame of reference. There is no illusive ranking or grading. The opinion of others has zero significance. I like the sound of that Mum. Self love, self care, self acceptance. Feeling Ok about myself. Perhaps she was trying to tell me it's about deciding for myself how much effort to make, how much money to spend, how much time to invest, and then being content with that. Nay, not content woman . . . happy! Spin on your toes, twinkle in your eye, loving the dress, loving myself, seriously not bothered what anyone thinks, happy! Holding my own.

Sweetheart

"Don't take me to Wigan Infirmary . . . I want to go to Bolton Royal" she firmly instructed the lady paramedic. Riding in the back of an ambulance was new to me, but the urgency of the situation shunted out any concerns about the correct protocol for accompanying one's mother to hospital. The paramedic kindly referred to my mother as sweetheart, which I knew she loved. Mum was safely strapped in place with what I presume was an oxygen mask secured to her face. The paramedic moved to the front of the vehicle and whispered just two words into the driver's ear "shut down". And off we bombed.

Those words about not going to Wigan Infirmary were Mum's last. She died later that day at Bolton Royal Hospital. I was both quietly pleased that she got her wish and amazed at the determination of a barely conscious, frail five stone woman, to speak at all. The memory of that day is truly dreadful in so many ways but Mum's comment always makes me smile. As does her insistence that she would not be eating frozen meals on wheels, thank you, and her timely exit just an hour before the first one was delivered.

Addled with dementia Dad knew just three things for certain. He had a stash of money; he had a wife he loved; I was keeping them both from him. My sister and

I battled valiantly to care for him in his own home but in the end we were resoundingly defeated by exhaustion and an insidious fear for Dad's and our own safety. The first time we stepped outside the care home without our beloved Dad, there was a private execution of my soul, so grotesque, so hideously final, so far beyond the engagement of language, that I dare not return to the story of it, not even with words on a page.

Bereaved, broken, and with Dad locked up in a home, partying had no appeal. Nor did living. Representing my parents at the Ruby Wedding Anniversary of a special aunt and uncle was important, and so we went, myself, my sister and our husbands. The old brass plaque hanging on my bedroom wall is embossed with the words of a poem composed by an ancient Warrior king. If I'm reading it right, the king is saying that it's a good idea to have a feast with others, even when walking through the valley of the shadow of death.

Sitting with my sister in a place that wasn't our deserted family home, the scary resuscitation bay of a hospital, the chapel of a crematorium, or the crowded communal lounge of a care home, was blissfully normal. Everyone was so alive. The warm faces of loving family members generated a comfort and joy. Cousins came to catch up, share their memories of our Mum and express their condolences. Los del Rio cheesily belted out the Macarena. Me and my best going out cardigan hit the dance floor and, for the first time in a long time, the sequinned bling stepped out from the darkness and into the light. And when you're in the light the bling will always shimmer.

It was just what I needed.

Purple and pearls

Elizabeth wore her purple cardigan with a string of pearls. A corded purple coat and silky scarf perfectly complimented her silver crown of hair. After the play I gave her a lift home to the little bungalow where she lived independently. As we entered the dark house late in the evening this tiny 90 year old lady, pottered off to "just check the rooms are ok".

"But shouldn't I be the one just checking the rooms are ok?" I asked. My question was met with her characteristic giggle. She stopped and turned towards me, simply smiled, cupped my face gently in her aging, arthritic hands and tenderly, silently, kissed my cheek, her eyes twinkling vibrantly with joy and love and life and a golden kind of energy.

In that exquisitely beautiful moment time seemed to melt into irrelevance. For a fleeting instant I felt as pure and lovely as the long forgotten five year old me again, wearing my favourite yellow cardigan with the blue bunny on it. The gates of heaven seemed to swing wide open and I was suddenly up close, perched in the doorway of a place outside of time which some call eternity, and the very eyes of God were looking out through hers and deep into mine. It was a profoundly surreal and private experience that left me utterly emotionally crushed and yet, at the same time, bouncing spiritually high.

Elizabeth was my mother-in-law, my spiritual Mum, and a spiritual Mum to many. She often told me: "No matter how old your children get you will never stop worrying about them". She was a woman who prayed for the needs and situations of those she loved every single day of her life and she confided: "the prayer list never gets any shorter".

Mum and I would talk trivia and trials in a single breath. We could leap from the blessings and agonies of motherhood, from fashion to faith, from pies to prayer.

Looking back now, I strongly believe that it was our shared ability to effortlessly surf from the shallows to the deeps and back again, in tandem, that really forged our unique connection. Goodnight 'extra' Mum and thank you.

The penny and the bun

A narrow band of gold outlines the upper rim of the spout. Another is drawn along the handle spine. A third and fourth encompasses the lid and the opening. A single pink rose sits centrally in a posy of flowers embedded on the round tea pot belly. From a pea sized hole three winding cracks sandwiched with hardened, yellow glue, radiate outwards. The outer of the sugar bowl is ridged, the inner smooth with more flowers. The tiny cups and saucers long since lost but I can see them now, on that marvellous day, all boxed up in readiness for the magical dolly's tea parties which would shortly follow.

She read me well, my other favourite auntie. And still, she calls me by my Sunday name and greets me with a giddy warm embrace, she knows my shoe size, my chequered history, my brewing preferences, and loves me still. Her lively chatter about the living and the dead conveys no difference in her tone, they are the same to her as ever was. Even now, in later life she always has something cooking on the stove, enough to feed an army, her home a constant buzz of visitors.

In my stormy seasons she advises me that all I can do is to hang onto my family and my faith. Her message carries weight as she has survived so many brutal storms herself. Hers is that quiet, private faith, characteristic of her generation. "We are the last generation with Victorian values" she confides. But she is no pushover, when the minister preached on resisting temptation she told him straight: "Wait until you're too old to be tempted, then you'll wish you never resisted."

Her cardigans are jewel colours, rich reds and greens and golds. "It's a rag without me in it" is her cheeky response to any compliment. Her dancing feet not quite so quick these days but her mind still dances well. She has opinions. Especially about those people who choose to live where the housing is cheaper and then commute to well paid city jobs. Should they whine about busy roads, poor public transport and the lack of seats on trains she has this no nonsense message. "You can't have the penny and the bun" she reasons "If you live more than ten miles away from where you work you're either in the wrong job or the wrong house."

Cardiology

5am. Toast, buttered. Tea, hot. Not a special recipe, but it tastes like heaven as an unfamiliar dawn breaks at the end of a long weary night of trying to sleep perched upright in a plastic chair. And always served with those smiling child-like eyes, and a hand gently pressing reassurance down into the soul through the ridge of the shoulder. A moment of inconsequential chit chat and a look which says I'm here, I'll help, you're safe, we'll sort it.

The head of a yellow pen peeps out just above the crisscross diamond stitched panel of her right pocket. A notepad, I think, hides in the left. A straggly thread holds the last of her five buttons tentatively. The ribbed cuffs are pushed upwards from both wrists, squeezing her slender forearms in a tightened grip. Their wiggly parallel rows emboss a tattooed bracelet onto her pale skin. Unborn pink scars silently cry out to be released from the unwelcome grasp. She does not heed them. The regal navy blue unintentionally compliments the paler cyan blue of her gloves and apron, and the rich natural warmth of the wool clashes rudely with the clinical coldness of the disposable plastic.

She helps patch up hearts which have broken, and diagnose those which are faulty, this cardiology nurse, working the room, in her navy blue cardigan. Floating through the chaos, bringing comfort and joy, and wheeling metal trolleys laden with stuff and things. When she listens she lowers herself down to the bed and looks you full in the eyes. She's reading your face as much as the chart and the blips and wiggles sliding hypnotically across the cryptic screen, sketching out the rhythm of your life.

She's knows what's what, but she won't say.

She knows the drill.

She's seen it all before.

She holds her tongue.

It's not her place to give the game away.

Each day she gets out of bed and chooses to come to work inside these walls. To care for these ungrateful, grumpy, sickly folks who are mostly miserable. To feed them, and talk to them, and listen to them. To clean up their blood and sick and wee and poo. All day. Day after day. And sometimes through the clanging crowded lonely night. It is beyond my understanding. Yet her angelic face, gentle way and slight of frame secretly belies her inner strength, push her too far, one time too many, and you will rue. You've met her, right?

She strokes his head, she holds his hand in hers, she takes his pulse. From across the ward another voice calls out to her. "Not again, Bernard." she snaps. "You're all right, you're all right."

8 Extras

"Live simply, dream big, love well, be fabulous." Supermarket cushion £4.99

Orphans

The rounded jar squats wide and low upon an inner shelf stopped loosely with a toady greying cork. Gifted from a friend of old its fine glass rim lips outwards in mock pout, sulking at my lack of care. The top nips waisted inwards, dropping onto sudden bussled hips. The belly holds a cast of orphaned buttons peering hopefully outwards through the muted glass.

Glossy black mushroom domes are stalked with silver loops. Flat discs pair up in bright pyjama pink. Chalky aspirin-white tablets are quartered with even punctured holes. Rounded sea shell bone is ridged and veined through with warming copper brown. Pearlised green moons are patched dark and light with slippery shadows. Vintage Mother of Pearl, brass and wood and leather sit quietly beside the noisy chrome and plastic. Some are clear as water, others dark or densely graded.

All are rescued.

A blunt chop through umbilical threads releases them from their garment before the rag bag makes its final claim upon them. Some escaped their bonds when tired out cotton strands unravelled their tenacious grip and dropped them to the ground in an untimely pinging bounce and scurry. Or down the sofa gorge along with pens and Bombay mix.

Tiny Tom Thumb sculptors hammer, chip and chisel into shape until the subject yields. Discs are carved with crests and channels then punctured with two holes, or four. Convex domes are formed and concave dishes scooped. Saucers, plates and platters are spun till good and round and neatly stacked upon each other.

These tiny sculptured works of art once adorned like costume jewellery. Highlighting the plain and lending mini episodes of drama to the dull. Blending subtly with the elaborate or sitting shyly in the background. Badges shouting statements of identity, I'm cute, I'm rugged, I'm earthy, I'm ethical, I'm trendy, I'm conventional, I'm not bothered.

Sunshine backlights those translucent jewel colours in the jar. Yellows tell their sherbert lemon lies. Orange glistens with barley sugar sweetness. Reds promise a hit of aniseed. Lime greens whisper of their melting chocolate inner. Each tempts the palette to believe that sweet sugar lies within. Like boiled sweets neatly jarred up in a retro sweet shop they wait to be chosen by the holy hand of rescue scooping them to freedom, and usefulness again.

Their original purpose was to marry up with a single pre-ordained button hole of perfect fit. To bring together twin opposites in reconciliation on that narrow band of common middle ground, and hold them in that place of closing over. Till they should will to be apart a while, yet still connected by the whole, in that natural ebb and flow of closeness and separateness whose tides ever shift within us all. To simply do their designated task and keep the wearer warm or cool as fits. They once played in a team, belonging to some long forgotten worn out thing, a jacket, shirt or blouse, a coat or cardigan. But now they are divorced and jobless, dancing in the disco jar with others of their kind, detached, displaced but beautiful and longing for a home.

Style without substance

I like pockets. Clothing without pockets is like a bath without bubbles, a disco without dancing, beans without toast, sand without sea, chips without fish . . . you get the picture. The only thing more disappointing than a garment without pockets is a garment with pretend pockets. Have you seen those fake pockets? I call them 'fockets' short for 'fake pockets'. But eyebrows were raised so I changed it to 'prockets' short for 'pretend pockets'.

They're pretty convincing. Some have zips, some have flaps with buttons. Presumably they have been added purely as a design detail. They look for all the world like a genuine pocket, fooling me once again, with the promise of securely housing my precious belongings.

When the moment comes to explore the pocket the strength of my reaction at that point depends how far I've travelled down the shopping-trying-buying-wearing timeline. In that first moment when the fastening on the fake pocket is undone to reveal there is in fact no pocket, I initially rationalise that it's been temporarily sewn up by the manufacturer to keep the shape of the garment. Or The Naughty Elves. You know, the ones who got kicked out of the North Pole. When they're not sewing up pockets, they travel the country mysteriously painting a letter 'I' in the middle of all the TO LET signs. Oh, you've seen them too. I can feel them secretly watching me trying to insert my hand in the 'focket' . . . er sorry I mean . . . 'procket', muffling their laughter at my bewilderment.

But my frustration with no pockets and 'prockets' only serves to increase my delight when I discover a really well thought out non-frumpy pocket. My absolute favourite pockets are the ones which are crafted so the opening sits almost invisibly along the side seam of the cardigan. Quirky zip tabs add a dressy feel and make locating and opening the pocket easy. Oh the joy. A rarely seen triumph of style and substance . . . and one in the eye for The Naughty Elves!

Doreen's secret

Doreen, a stylish pensioner with thick white hair and an impeccable taste for hand crafted jewellery, well remembers hand knitting cardigans for her family. When she knitted a cardigan for herself she would create two deep pockets, and stitch each of them onto the front panels just below waist level. Next, taking some very fine wool and fine knitting needles she would knit a third smaller pocket. The dimensions of this creation were given careful consideration for it would be entrusted to house Doreen's most important treasure; her credit card.

This little pocket would then be stitched onto the inside of the cardigan. Doreen would carefully place it behind one of the visible pockets where her credit card would lie flat and undetected behind the 'real' pocket.

She confided: "These days I just cut the toe end out of an old sock, slip my credit card into it and then firmly attach it to the inside of my cardigan with a large safety pin. There's sometimes a bit of rummaging about to get the card out to pay for things in the shop, I have to think ahead so as not to hold up the queue at the till."

The party cardy

Swallows, or maybe Swifts, I never could tell the two apart. Showing off for all the world. Look at me, look at me! Swooping and diving energetically, efficiency gains the least of their concern. We stopped and leaned against each other to watch this private air show. Exchanging wide eyed little head nods and broad wordless grins, like only really good friends can. The uneven, rocky path ran along the perimeter of an immense farmer's field. We glanced up at intervals to check for rogue hawthorn branches leaning out to spike us. Our shoulders were hunched in mutual downward gazes as we watched our footing, for fear the unpredictably lumpy earth would kettle us over on our ankles.

Over brooks and stiles we wandered like a little band of characters from a Rupert Bear Annual. An open village church welcomed us in for a brief oaken sit within the coolness of its yard thick stone walls. Next stop, the Inn of Englandshire, all foamy dark ale and roast beef dinners. We chatted our grown up chat for a while, sharing truths we could tell no other. Surely trusting for, and then receiving, understanding, warmth and kindness. Then off we trogged into that grassy summer day, wandering for a few more miles till tea time.

Back at the car we changed our boots in readiness for a special evening meal out together. We girls fluffed up our hair a bit, baby wiped our sweaty faces and mutually rationalized our lack of grooming after a long sticky walk. My friend's waist-tied walking fleece was quickly bagged. Then, with all the flair of a stage magician, out she whipped a floaty white cloud of a cardigan. She gave it a little shake then slipped it lightly over her shoulders. Flicking her hair upwards and outwards with both hands, she released it from where it was trapped inside the collar of the cardigan. The wispy summer knit fell dramatically down, draping dress-like just above her knees. A transparent feminine froth enveloped her. In one smooth move she was transformed from serious explorer to elegant night on the town girl.

Silky white threads looped and weaved rhythmically. Shaping into neat sun crested waves then rolling out in ever increasing frequency before crashing onto a frenzied coastline of delicate knotted cogs and scallops. Here and there a flimsy snag waved its wispy unravelled fingers above the surface of it all. Denser crocheted strands were tied loosely at the centre, bringing the two front panels together in a casual, flirty embrace. Their ends brushed downwards like narrow ribbons before falling onto three tightly woven oval discs. Each disc composed of a hundred or more close concentric threads stitched shoulder to shoulder creating a solid button-like mass.

In turn each crocheted disc was weighted like the pendulum of a grandfather clock. Three miniature conker like beads were threaded on their necks. They swung and crashed about randomly as she walked, each competing with the other for space and rhythm, dancing for attention with each step, but their movement made no sound at all.

9 Life in Cardigans

"Snow falls gently on my roof,
years have flown by since my youth,
winter's here, it's dark and cold,
lasting memories from of old.
Snow on the roof,
fire in the hearth,
I'll hold my loved ones here in my heart,
though seasons change and people too,
I will remember all of you."

From the song Snow on the Roof by Bob and Val Fraser.
www.bobfrasermusic.com

The Christmas cardy

Softly waving candlelight reveals a thousand flecks of twinkling woven gold, once hidden by darkness down among the textured shades of forest greens. Lights and darks mingle together in a silky, sparkly cheek to cheek tango. Drapes and folds fall earthwards, their softly pointed tips touching down lightly onto neatly papered parcels. Bold tartans and mirrored silvers piled one upon the other, all topped off with red nosed reindeer packages and woolly hatted penguin shapes.

No dangly belts, fuss or tassels. Neat three quartered sleeves with bracelet cuffs stop well above the action. Perfectly designed for peeling spuds, pouring gravy, and washing up mountains of pots and pans. Loose and fine and light too, because the kitchen gets so very hot. An oh so Christmassy cardigan gifted from my oh so very own Queen of Christmas.

The mega mix fills up the house with favourites yet again, sleigh riding me giddily into Christmas. And the Queen of Christmas squeals excitedly, ho-ho-ing in through the door upon her snow trimmed, red suited arrival. Bringing bags and bags of simply fabulousness. Too generous. Too generous by far. But she will not be told. She won't y'know. And we love her all the same and then some more. She's been counting down and stashing stuff since August, it's no secret. She's the rarest of lovelies; a dichotomous mix of being wholly adult while simultaneously being wholly child.

The song goes on: 'Joy and pain run side by side, like ebb and flow of time and tide'. I'm blessed to love a lot of people, and so joy and pain are always playing out their melody. To avoid feeling pain is to avoid feeling love, and to avoid feeling love is to avoid feeling joy, and to avoid feeling joy, is to avoid feeling anything, and to avoid feeling, is to avoid being.

Harris Tweed

Mingling among the elegant camel-coated ladies and smart shirted Gareth Malone types I see a giggling family, group-hugging their Mum in a totally touchable fluffy pink gillet. This is the January Sale. Hidden away in the far corner of Bents award winning garden centre lies an extraordinary library of comforting, cuddly, cardigans.

Skipping excitedly to the Aran section I have to touch them all. I want to own them all, live in them all. Designed for deepest winter their weight and thickness affords protection from the bleakest weather. The naturally beautiful range of knitwear delivers a heart warming, Christmassy comfort and joy. Intricate, rustic patterns weave and bob their way from shoulder to hip in a traditional three dimensional relief. Rich coffee colours soothe with a calm natural earthiness which feels so right.

A splash of pleated tartan skirts attracts the attention of two tiny ladies who then discuss the great merit of said items. A range of classic cut jackets and coats is being tried on by Mums and their daughters. I notice the men's shirts, winter woollies and golfing gear is being calmly browsed by a selection of handsome salt and pepper haired guys. One or two stylish twenty-something men eye the incredibly smart Harris Tweed jackets and matching waistcoats.

I'm distracted in every direction. The fire engine red sale stickers are pulling me this way and that. I've learned, much to my delight, year on year, that this particular 50% off promise is the real deal. The store is buzzing with bargain hunters who seem to have learned the same lesson. I text my sister to confirm that I am now officially a boring old fart.

With less than 48 hours remaining of the year a little panic sets in, as midnight on December 31st signifies the alleged end of all high calorie consumption for me. It's my time honoured tradition to begin all diets with a blow out and so I decide to smugly review my bargain purchases in the nationally acclaimed restaurant. Mr Cardigan joins me for a nice pot of tea and we get to grips with a flapjack the size of a railway sleeper.

We successfully dodge the hand-made chocolates and trendy Christmas decorations but fold at the half price table mats. Leaving the crowd behind we sheepishly return to the sanctuary of our home. We are greeted by the pungent aroma of boys, our front door left unlocked and half a dozen dishevelled young men eating pizza and playing the World of War Craft game across two decorating tables. And none of them are wearing Harris Tweed.

The joiner

The joiner was the first to know. He knelt on my kitchen floor, his head buried deep inside a cupboard. His tatty blue cardigan with holes in the elbows and frayed cuffs jarred in comparison to his substantial, purpose made work trousers fitted with large zipped pockets and protective knee pads. I found myself wondering where I might get a pair and how much they might cost.

Emerging from the cupboard he began trotting off a stream of decimal figures and incomprehensible calculations. A well extended retractable metal tape measure was brandished in the air like a thin, bendy sword, presumably for dramatic effect. With some satisfaction he pressed the release button, instantly propelling the thin slice of metal into a rattling downward whizz. Like a non-stop express train bombing through a station it passed through the lightened grip of his calloused fingers at a frightening speed before disappearing into its casing, momentarily putting my teeth on edge at the thought of his severed digits.

"There's enough room to fit another unit into that void" he said with the eyes of an outhouse rat, as if he were the first explorer to discover the dark cave which I had de-gunked just hours earlier. "That would give you a lot more storage space" he grinned, his nodding head mentally adding each extra pound to the invoice.

Without any great thought the response left my mouth in a dry, flat, matter of fact way. There was no drama in my tone, no hint of a dilemma. It was as if someone else spoke and I heard them say: "We don't need any extra storage space ... there's just the two of us now." And there it was. Out in the open. For absolute certainty. One of the most significant changes of my adult life. Announced without the ringing taps of spoon against crystal. Without introduction, explanation or carefully crafted speech. Without a cheering crowd. Just me, the joiner and the kitchen sink.

Decades of feeding and housing, caring and sharing, driving and delivering, loving and listening, thinking and weeping, dreaming and praying. My involvement has varied in intensity with each stage of my children's lives but this was the first time I had ever considered each of them to be fully, truly, never-to-return independent, and my work completed.

"There's just the two of us now." It was an intense realisation. A shift in who I am. And yet I had inadvertently announced my life changing news to a passing workman whose name I can't even remember. There was no pause in our business conversation to mark that unnoticed moment in which I knew I had become one half of "just the two of us". No affirming hand shake, elegant champagne reception or hefty redundancy cheque. Just a stranger kneeling on the kitchen floor, talking about wooden plinths and asking for decisions about end panels.

Disturbance in the force

Looking out across the night something felt wrong. This wrongness gasped and choked for air in a deep place within me which I cannot easily name. Dialogue was not its channel, or even words, neither were feelings, nor thoughts. Something other, something primal, unquantifiable, unidentified. Yet wholly tangible to some as yet unproven sense, alarming and threatening, like the faint burning scent of thick black smoke in the distance, unseen but real.

Car headlights flickered past sending thin yellow beams of light dancing around within the thickly doubled glass. The wrongness shouted at me from the silence and wild tears burst out of me in an anxious, shaky protest. But I did not heed them. The bus shelter across the road where he would sometimes sit was lit up like a tiny, empty stage screaming for its player to appear. I should have phoned him. I should have.

The knock on the door was just as you would expect. A plain clothed introduction, the formal presenting of a badge. Polite enquiries as to name. A realisation of seriousness. Hushed invitations to the lounge, to sit, to have tea. Questions, scribbled notes, too many. Yes the bag is his, and the old school cardigan stuffed within it. Straining to remember details through the soupy tang of shock and all the while the wrongness shouting at me, I should have phoned him. I should have.

Four years pass.

It's that ward again, the one I do not like. I leave late. Mine is the last car here. Darkness greys her grief quietly around me and a decision to cope springs forth. What-ifs peck and snatch hungrily at what sanity remains yet I survive the drive home. I sleep with the lights on in two rooms, more anguish, more not knowing, but tiredness wins for now.

And then the phone.

From far away, his sentence served, his life established and secure, past mistakes now just a blip. To enquire, and wish well, and promise to visit, and say goodnight. To offer comfort and make contact in that precise moment of anguish of which he knew nothing, as no one knew.

How did he know?

How did he know he should have phoned, then did?

King or common man

He's a great catch, a handsome man of noble character, and I know him well. His punchy zip up cardigan falls just below that location in the middle of the body which men refer to as their waist. Classic carbon black apart from two broad stripes of cream in a consistent width. Each travels down from its starting position at the neck line, across broad shoulders, down strong arms before halting with a reliable, satisfying stop at the cuffs.

An identical pair of pockets mirror each other. Discreet diagonal openings lie symmetrically low across the front panels. Their position affords a comfortable resting place for his blokey hands and sometimes tired limbs. The fine knit rolls up into a tight cylinder in his rucksack, appearing only when needed to afford him a helpfully thin layer of warmth without bulk, ideally suited to this muscled member of the species. The slight upstand of the rib knit collar lies just as easily against a dressy cotton shirt as it does against a sloppy round necked t-shirt.

His cardigan does not deliver the protective, caressing cuddles, which hand knitted woollies lovingly direct without reservation, to the irresistible cuteness of the young. Neither does it give him the needy options of warmth and style that women's cardigan's demand. Nor is this the sloppy food stained cardigan of the aged man. Who, in final resignation to those failing joints, which lack the strength and flexibility to manoeuvre a jumper up over the head then down the body, surrenders style and reluctantly returns to the elasticated, unstructured garb of early childhood.

A rare sight, this entirely masculine cardigan so adequately reflects the inner qualities of the wearer. Like the broad cream stripes he is of consistent character, a man who starts things well and always finishes them with flair. Like the classic monochrome colours he has a timeless quality. His strong values of honesty, hard work and sacrifice underpin every day of his life. Like the versatility of the stand up collar he is as comfortable with king or common man. Like the fine knit of the fabric he offers a breathable open handed brand of warmth when needed, but never stifles with over bearing suffocation.

And like those balanced well positioned pockets, he deliberately puts himself in a place where he can give an ever ready support to those of us who are fortunate enough to live within the reach of his world. Those who are tired he will help, those who have fallen down he holds up.

Yes, he's a great catch.

The hardy cardy

My third invitation to a foreign holiday this year, lucky me. Except in my family 'foreign holiday' is usually code for a painting and decorating party. Or a house move. Or a cleaning party. Or a tip run. Or anything that involves dust, muck and mire. A bonus inclusion is the semi-permanent loaning and occasional permanent loss of my tools and DIY equipment. And yet I love it, and they know I do. Just as much, if not more, than a foreign holiday, hence the nick name.

Hair drenched with sweat, face blotched red, hands and arms speckled with crusts of dried emulsion, and the hem of my scruffy painting trousers soaked with carpet shampoo. Forensically de-dusting every pot and noodle in a freshly re-wired kitchen from top to bottom. Carefully cutting out shapes and squiggles and patching up multi scuffed wallpaper like an eight foot tall mind game. Scraping and painting and wiping and washing my way into a delicious, all hands to the pump, purposeful OCD high.

The hardy cardy is on, then off, then on again, as body temperature see-saws from the work. The dark mix of cheap yet durable manmade fibres is generously slimed from waist to hem with wallpaper paste. Fluffed rough as a badger's backside all over. Snagged nearly to shreds on the seat area, and worn thin from the frequent taking of tea breaks with my sit upon temporarily resting on any bare floor, packing box, door step or industrial size tin of paint.

That missing button matters not, the remaining three work well enough. Cheap but not especially cheerful. Supermarket bought, mass produced in Taiwan methinks. Not a natural fibre in sight. Machine stitched seams all firmly intact in spite of multiple tuggings. And two belt loops remain fixed firmly into the side seams at the waist, though the belt for which they fit is long since gone, no doubt scooped up and binned. Rough to the touch, papery from too many hot washes. School uniformish in style, verging on the Mumsy, but still useful.

Flasks of tea and shop bought butties, sometimes crisps, we share them all. Acceptance and belonging, purpose and meaning, fill these filthy, funny days. To love and then, to be allowed to demonstrate my love in this tangible messy, minging way gives bliss beyond Barbados.

10 Cardigan Clocking

"There is no bad weather, only bad clothing." Reputed to be a Scandinavian saying.

A quiet corner

"Could we eat in a quiet corner please?"

"Of course." The pub restaurant is, for now, empty. We're led to a table that is neither in a corner, nor quiet, but one which is located next to the gurgling coffee machines, nearest to the kitchen access and therefore, I cynically deduce, the shortest distance for the waiter to walk. And situated about two metres from a long bay of tables reserved for thirty members of the University of the Third Age. (An organisation where mature folks meet to exchange wisdom and skills.) I restate my requirements: "Could we have a table in a quiet corner please?"

"Certainly" he says, indicating to exactly the same table again. We roll our eyes, sit down and order.

Our mains arrive, along with the aforementioned thirty University of the Third Age folks. They inch and shuffle their way noisily along the tight perimeters of the long table until, barring a few trips to the loo and the bar, they settle down to order. Our quiet table in the corner just became the ringside seat to a significant birthday celebration of some fairly uninhibited lively older folks. The drinks flow and the sound of glasses clinking can just be heard above the cackling. They look to be having quite a lot of fun, very possibly more than we are having.

As they arrive I notice that the majority of the women and several of the men are wearing an impressive assortment of cardigans. I count twenty. Mild irritation morphs into outright curiosity. From my vantage point in the 'quiet corner' I'm able to observe their behaviour like a scientist studying mice in a lab. It's a shifting summer evening in the north of England and, for a woman writing a book about cardigans, a God given opportunity to compare the men and women's cardigan related behaviour. As experiments go, I couldn't have planned it better myself.

As my mental bets are placed I sit back with a second glass of Rioja and hope they do not notice me, noticing them. One of the men is wearing an impressively thick traditional Aran cardigan, over a shirt and tie. At the back of his neck the double ribbed knit collar of the cardigan sits higher than the collar of the shirt, this creates a molly-coddling scarf like effect and no doubt affords him serious protection from draughts and chills. Every button is fastened tight and the sleeves and cuffs are pulled firmly down over the backs of his hands. I surmise that his is the thickest and heaviest cardigan in the room and I confidently wager it will be off and on the back of the chair before the end of the first course.

The food arrives and they're all over it like seagulls round a chip. I guess wrong. He keeps it on, and buttoned up, from soup course to dessert right through to the cheese and biscuits and after dinner mints. I watch expectantly for the entire evening but not a drop of sweat dampens his brow. Perhaps a love of cardigans, much like colour blindness, has been carried by the female of his species, then passed to this unsuspecting male. Or, I rationalise, perhaps the poor chap has a thyroid problem, or an un-ironed shirt.

I'm relieved when my predictions for the other three men prove to be entirely accurate. They do not disappoint me. Sure enough their fairly dull, sensibly coloured cardigans are all removed and placed on the backs of their chairs by the time their plates are empty. And I'm intrigued to note that there they remain for the rest of the evening. Their cardigans are simply worn upon arrival, taken off at some early point during the meal, and then replaced for departure. The cardigan action for the men's team is predictable, and enviously unfussy.

The women's team are far more entertaining. They sport a stunning array of cardigans in all manner of colours, textiles and styles. Some look like they have been carefully chosen to match their outfit, others are trusted favourites pragmatically thrown on simply for warmth. One is an intricately patterned Fair Isle hand knitted beauty, each tiny stitch sitting logically next to the other in a fantastical geometric design. Another resembles a shaggy grey hound, its wiry fur highlighted with a brush of white at the tips. The black and purple chequerboard hem of another hangs like a half deflated Guy Fawkes on the back of the chair. A gold lurex shrug is tied high up on the waist, its long ties falling decadently down. You know the sort it belongs to, one of those canny women who whips out a lipstick after a meal and applies it swiftly at the table without the aid of a mirror.

I observe closely as many of the women systematically work their way through four levels of warmth and back again. On and fully buttoned, on though unbuttoned, on the shoulders only, and finally, fully removed. I resist the overwhelming urge to cheer as my obsessively researched theories about cardigans are played out in multiple confirmations.

Without exception all the women arrive wearing their cardigans. Throughout the starter most are casually unbuttoned. By the end of the main course the food in their bellies is generating heat and their body temperatures are rising. One by one, arms are being awkwardly slipped out of sleeves. Apologies are discharged gracefully, while trying to avoid elbowing neighbouring diners. Some cardigans remain draped over shoulders, while others are fully removed and placed, to hand, over the backs of chairs. Only one person in the group of thirty, a woman, takes her cardigan and hangs it on the coat stand a few metres away, but by the time dessert arrives she has retrieved it and places it across her lap.

From my track side seat I'm glued to the action. The unscripted, cardigan related manoeuvres of the evening roll out before me in a thoroughly entertaining live race . . . a running radio commentary plays in my head . . .

". . . and they're off, and it's Pink Lady in the lead, Pink Lady in the lead, her fork is down and she's moving fast, she's cleared the back of the chair and the cardigan is draped stylishly, look at her go! Now it's Glamour girl coming up on the inside, she's got one arm out, now the other, oh no she's stuck . . . and it's Gentleman Jim to the rescue! He's coming up behind her, look at him move over those jumps! Oh no Fearless Frank overtakes him, it's Fearless Frank, they're neck and neck, shoulder to shoulder, oh I think that was push, but he's got there first, Fearless Frank pulls off the sleeve, Glamour girl in the lead. Dainty Doreen is coming up fast on the inside, and she's got hers over the back of the chair too. Next it's Rum Lad, quickly followed by Nancy's Friend, Nancy's Friend in the lead, she's over the finish line, and coming in last it's Reserved Rita!"

In between courses there is much female shuffling about. Some of the ladies go to the loo, and others stand up and move along the table to chat. Some of the cardigans are back on, then off again! Throughout the evening I observed an average adjustment/removal rate of eight cardigan adjustments per woman compared to just less than two cardigan adjustments per man.

Just saying.

Women of substance abuse

Filter coffee and tea mostly, sometimes cake and pastries, frequently chocolate and occasionally wine and cigarettes. These are the women of socially acceptable substance abuse. Warm buttery croissants flake and crumble their way lightly onto the flimsy paper plate balanced upon the web of an upturned hand. The severity of her black polo neck jumper is softened by the warm autumnal rust of her cardigan. Slender dark arms are capped by short sleeves flaring out just above the elbow, and I make a mental note of this flattering idea. She seems to be running the show and gently directing us towards the selection of cereals and yoghurt. Top brass and underlings alike stand shoulder to shoulder, buzzing greedily around the complimentary croissants and cinnamon rolls. Coffee in hand I find a seat and plonk my bag down onto the chair beside me, territorially reserving a space for my colleague who I know will be arriving a little late.

On the second row a cross over fuchsia pink cardigan clashes boldly with a delicate willow patterned scarf swirled loosely around the neck. It passes through a tunnel of dense dark hair before emerging into the light, forming a vast swathe of fabric, draped in concentric folds like the grand curtain above the stage at the Royal Theatre. Two seats away a fine beige cardigan disappears against the fleshy body of a tired pale woman. Behind her on the next row a zing of lime green reflects the morning sun creating a glowing atomic energy bubble around its wearer. Three seats to the right a long streak of factory produced, dull white acrylic engulfs a tall skinny woman in a rubbery crackle of static shocks, two waterfall drapes point harshly to the ground like long jowls, dragging her fragile features cruelly downwards.

Space between the rows of chairs is tight. While seated the knee caps of my stubby little legs jam up against the unyielding metal framed chair in front of me. Upon standing to welcome and applaud the first speaker the spacial dynamics alter surprisingly. I feel the flabby apron of my tummy ledged awkwardly on the back of said chair, and a greasy crumb of croissant regret rudely kicks the big backside of my conscience. Transparent white braids delicately outlining the peplum of my best work cardigan frill out like a little tutu dancing over the edge of a Juliet balcony at eventide. Three quarter length sleeves are cuffed with their own little frill and matching white braid forming a clumsy trio of unsynchronized ballerinas. A satin ribbon beds four glossy, deliberately mis-matched buttons, and I'm feeling all last season M&S, but I persuade myself it's a style classic with plenty of life left in it.

Prompted by the cow shed effect the wide lady sitting in front of me cautiously slides off her sloppy banana yellow boyfriend cardigan. Her top half rotates 180 degrees turning to drape it over the back of her chair where my tummy is having a little rest. My booted calves are already pressed hard against the seat of my own chair and I can't move back any further. I offer a sort of half smile and half squat, momentarily withdrawing my tummy from her chair. Her invasive chunky number robs a further two inches off my limited space. High velcrocity fibres have trapped and threaded a good haul of her wispy broken hair into the open weave, along with specks of lint and the odd fluffy wisp of duck down, strayed from her duvet or Ralph, the friendly pet duck I imagine her to have rescued as a chick. I want to pick all the bits out monkey like, one by one, and then step out into the green city court yard winking at me through the hazy Edwardian glass, hold my breath, close my eyes, and give it a blinking good shake.

The lady in the striking black and tan combo holds the floor. One delegate's head dives down to retrieve a notepad from a bag, momentarily breaking the straight pattern of the row, before bobbing back up again. Across the room another bobs down then up again, then another, like Ralph's duck family feeding in the morning swell. Minor adjustments are made to hair and clothes and chairs and sitting positions until eventually everyone settles down into their own silence.

A stone coloured longline cardigan, Phase Eight I'll wager, gives a clear presentation on the ins and outs of reputation management, before launching into the darkness of media law. Edge to edge front panels fall open to reveal a ruched brown top, visually dividing her torso into three vertical bands of contrasting colour. My inner voices debate the argument for and against buttons, and discuss what length of coat she must need to cover its ample length, when really I ought to be cobbling together some notes about plagiarism.

84 steps down to the tube station, and I'm growing more uncomfortable with every shallow breath of the long descent. Firmly I tell myself that I can do this because my grandad was a miner and I am really a rabbit, I am really a rabbit. The train back north cradles me with a gentle rock. Familiar, fast and smooth and reassuringly on the ground, not under it. That deep satisfaction which comes from escaping the metropolis, heading home, mission accomplished, stills my jumbled thoughts like a kind hand on my shoulder. Settling down with a kit Kat and a good lid of Methodist tea I'm disturbed by two men arguing loudly in the seat across from mine.

A lively public competition about which of them had travelled the world most played out across three southern counties. The taller one is a funny onion who would clearly mither a nest of rats. By the time we pass through Birmingham he's in the lead and the whole carriage is silently rooting for the under-dog. Not least of all, I conclude, because he is wearing an exceptionally inviting cardigan. The crisp cotton collar of his checked shirt is buttoned smartly down. Affectionately nuzzling against the sharp up stand leans the soft deep collar of a stunning rustic hand knit befitting of the finest gentleman farmer on his way to Sunday lunch with the Mayor. If he'd squeezed a Black Faced Welsh Mountain sheep and two sticks out of his leather brief case and began knitting directly from its fleece I wouldn't have blinked an eye.

I drop my bags and throw my formal jacket over the newel post. Loo then brew before my scruffy house cardigan welcomes me like an old furry friend, its sagging pockets and bobbled fibres judge me not. Coat like proportions envelope me with a warm beddy embrace, and what remains of the evening closes in around me. And even if I should doze off during the crucial bits of Lewis, it will never tell tales on me because that is what it secretly hopes will happen.

Dinner and a show

Stubbing out the cigarette with repeated jabs her chin jutted upwards. A plume of grey smoke left her pursed mouth like a kettle spouting steam. Slipping into the line ahead of us she injected an ember of borrowed warmth in among the black leather jackets of that chilly autumn day. Zesty orange cashmere picked up the colour of three plate sized flowers pasted brightly onto a wallpaper dress. Flame gold hair was flat iron straight with wispy uneven ends trailing off like brush fibres disappearing into the knit. Almond toed patent leather stilettos, in yet more orange, completed the candle burning at both ends effect. Pairs of stewards inspected the contents of our open bags, then herded us down and down, to sit under the vast expanse of the balcony improbably suspended above us.

Powder blue lace strained over the severe right angle of a forcefully folded arm. The stretch floral weave opened up reluctantly revealing a clinical grey sling grinning through a gaping pattern of distorted roses. Ties were fastened tightly at the empire line creating a lob sided bolster across the upper body like a new born babe pulled in close to feed under the cover of a blanket. One sleeve played host to a lucky unbroken arm gripping a plastic glass of sloshing white wine, elbow raised high in wildly animated freedom, its owner giggling at herself. The other sleeve was, for now, redundant and cunningly tucked away somewhere deep within the sanctuary of the shrug cardigan.

The curtain rose. Her relaxed hand brushed across his palm. For a second it was partly enclosed by his fingers in a deliberate loving embrace before gently passing through them and sliding out of the other end as she moved away. Their touch lasted only a moment as they passed each other under cover of the dim house lighting in the aisle. She didn't break her step and neither did he. They looked beyond each other, staring ahead and awkwardly avoiding eye contact, even more so than strangers might. As far as I could tell no words were spoken. Her calf length cardigan was undone and its flowing corners flapped out behind her like the long sheer veil of a bride running away. They each continued on their respective ways, eventually stopping to sit beside another. My eyes were following the cardigan at that secret moment of convergence, the theatre was darkened, no one else saw, I wished I hadn't either.

Harsh stage uplighters illuminated his mop of blonde hair and angelic young face. A capital letter in white was appliqued onto one panel of his pocket-less navy blue cardigan which stood flat as an ironing board against him. He sang silky love songs to a girl wearing a mustard yellow cardigan, a1950s style skirt, ankle socks and flat shoes. Will-they-won't-they tension played out in a classic three act drama of dance and song. The cardigans span and jived and doo-wapp showaddywaddied their way all over the stage before slowing down for that final moon-lit smooch. And the audience sighed "Aaaaah".

11 In Any Case

"Strength and honour are her clothing and she is confident about the future." Proverbs 31:25 Common English Bible

The quinquennial frock

'Sorry sis can't do coffee after work today three of us sent home sick been stuck in bed since yesterday xx' read the incoming text message on my phone. We meet in a cafe hidden deep inside a large mill shop. Colourful clothes catch my eye on the way in. But my sis, who is way more trendy than me, always warns: "Don't buy anything in here, it's all old lady stuff".

Regressing into the comfort of childhood patterns this quickly became our standing joke. I play the rebellious younger sister and she the wiser older one. Sensible slippers purchased before she arrived and revealed over coffee generated a great reaction: "No! They're Granny slippers!" she objected "take them back! What have I told you about this place?" We laughed so much it was worth every penny.

But today big sis was 'stuck in bed'. And I had sunk into a sulky no-frock-for-the-party mood. The formal annual Valentine bash often caught me frock-less, in spite of happening at exactly the same time every year. In previous years I'd worn the same black frock three times, a borrowed red frock, and a black and red frock twice. Boring. Borrowed. Old. Five years old in fact. Whaaat? It's been five years since I bought a new frock? Oh man, this was all kinds of wrong. I looked at my watch. The mill shop was still open. She would never know.

Four times I trudged around that blinking women's department skennin the racks with a face like a robber's dog. In mild panic I looked out for anything that would pass for a half decent frock which I could actually wear outside of the house. Nothing. She was right. I should have listened. It was all old lady stuff. I had to admit defeat, go home and face the same old same old.

But before turning to leave, I paused. Praying for a party dress seems disgracefully shallow but without thinking about it properly I just chunnered in the vague direction of God in a ridiculous juvenile whine: "C'mon God, can I just have a pretty new dress for the party please? Can I? Pleeeese? I'm so weary of being the girl in the wrong dress."

Returning for my fifth lap of the women's department I walked past a long rack of oddments. Something made me stop, turn around and reach in. And there it was. The dress of my dreams. Delicate narrow ribbons of satin swept from the neckline to the hem, the gaps between them widening on the way down. Fine black mesh danced out from between the ribbons. It was exquisite and fitted perfectly.

Narrow shoulder straps held the whole feminine creation firmly in place. But without the cover of sleeves my strong but wobbly upper arms were a sight that could frighten a police horse. This was bad. Further frantic searching turned up a little shrug cardigan and I was rescued from revealing said wobbly flesh. The black jersey picked up on the colour of the mesh nicely and the lightweight fabric added to the flouncy feel of the outfit. Its soft cuffs flared out from the elbow and a tie fastening hung long and loose at the front. Knotted together with the long black satin dress belt they cinched the frock in to create a flattering, reasonably woman-shaped, empire line.

It felt fabulous! But more than that. The outfit did what well designed, well made clothes can sometimes do best . . . teach an old bird not to give up on being a girl just yet. The astonishing reminder that God still hears my prayers and is working to bless me, even in trivial matters, was an energizing bonus feature!

In heaven I'll wear Jaeger

The horizontal stripes of black and green/black were so subtle that, in certain lights, the whole cardigan looked black. In my head I thought it matched everything else I owned, which was probably a mistake. It was fine and light, yet very warm. The knit was smooth and a winter coat could be slipped easily over it without any drag, bunching or tightness on the arms. Two sturdy pockets graced the front. The generous length fell well below my bottom, which I thought was too big, but now know it was just a bottom. The classic style felt elegant and flattering. This was my very first Jaeger cardigan and I adored it.

Donated to me by a well-off cousin it had arrived in a bag of designer cast offs. The fabrics were of a high quality and the construction and weight of the garments impressive. Drooling over a fine concealed zip sewn invisibly into the seam of a lined tartan skirt was a fashion high point. This was classy stuff. I'd never seen anything like it before.

The Jaeger cardigan was prized above all the other items in the bag. I wore it often. Paired with black jeans and a nice blouse it had the fashion clout to thoroughly convince me of my own trendiness. I washed it and wore it and washed it and wore it. With the benefit of hindsight I can see I gave it a right hammering. But never a bobble appeared, nor a stitch or button came loose. It kept its colour, it kept its shape. I fell in love with its tough high performance delivery.

Until a sleeve was chewed up by the washing machine. I was peeved to my core! Repair was fruitless. My Jaeger was destroyed, but the passing of time has not faded the memory of its awesomeness. On the contrary, I just may have sainted it.

Sixteen pence and a polo mint

Mogshade: Neither day nor night. It's that funny in between time. I soak in the bath because I'm tired and tummy achy or just plain peopled out. I emerge feeling too warm and floppy to get dressed into restrictive day clothes but not quite tired enough to give up and admit it's time to sink into bed. It's far too early to wear pyjamas plus I don't want to look like an old crock either.

Or it's a day off. But not that day out shopping or sight seeing or lunching with mates kind of a day off. No, this is a proper full on day off spent entirely at home. A day off from people. Not going out, not even to the corner shop to buy a stamp for that birthday card I really should get posted today. Selfish. A day off from the tedious, fiddly application of makeup, especially from the draining concentration which comes from poking around your eyelashes with a vicious brush full of black gloopy mascara. And seriously, why bother when there are still a few clumps left on from yesterday? Minger. And that demanding unruly pet nesting atop my head which I usually refer to as my hair, now so accurately represents the scrambled contents of my brain. It's doing that Bob

Geldof on a bad day thing again. My tired blotchy face skens like a bucket of whelks. My limbs are heavy and cold and I long to be sewn into my vest for the winter and settle down with a good lid of tea.

Or maybe it's one of those vague nagging I-need-to-stay-at-home-to-catch-up kind of a day. There's bits to shave and pluck and trim and wax. Post, admin and shredding to do. Junk emails to delete. Passwords to change. Laundry to wash and bedding to strip. Stuff to sort and file and ditch. That claggy rat of drain hair is blocking up the tray of the shower cubicle again and needs urgently hoyking out. At the end of the day it can feel like I haven't stopped for a minute and yet I'm not entirely sure what I've achieved. That sinking feeling born from low productivity nips at my heels but I kick it away by calling this my catch up day.

Soft stretchy fabric in black velour fits comfortably around my unattractive wobbly bits. Three pink zips add interest along the pockets and up the front. Tamzin Outhwaite jogs in hers during the opening credits of New Tricks. Cardigan shaped for sure, but perhaps more of a top for doing sports. I like it, it's second hand, she gave it to me. My sister, not Tamzin Outhwaite.

Hand me downs have stories, and I like stories. And bargain, it bears that number on the label, not seen for many years, which may be spoken of out loud. She left sixteen pence and a polo mint in the pocket. I told you hand me downs have stories. Comfortable black leisure pants thrown on, and the outfit is acceptable for days off and mogshade.

Fire

Fire. Fence posts. Curry. Bleach. Paint. Grease. Mascara. Washers. Dryers. Car doors. Cats. Dogs. Red wine. Hair dye. Felt pens. Biros and baby sick.

Each one of these rogues has ruined and robbed me of a cardigan. A perfectly good, painfully paid for cardigan. Bought on purpose. Now they all lie tangled in the landfill. Coiled around with compressed litter. Time locked and forever lost. Discarded and forgotten like missed opportunities, like the boys who didn't notice me, like the teams I wasn't picked for and the smiles I never gave.

Irreversible damage is unlike wear and tear. You know; the ordinary plucks, pills and bobbles of every day that must simply be withstood, endured, lived with. Loose threads and little snags which can be carefully knotted tightly back in place. Gradual thinning at the elbow which can be patched and protected, given the will and the wherewithal. Creeping erosion at the cuff which can be concealed with a tuck and a turn back, if sleeve length suffices. Brews and stews and spills and ills that can be biologically vanished away without a trace. Vibrant colour which fades to a shade, though a paler portion of itself, still bonny. Fallen buttons that move graciously aside for another that does the job just as well. Sagging pockets that can be, well, quietly left to sag, in a welcoming hammock for the hand.

No, these villains are not at all like wear and tear. They lay waiting to ambush me. To mock me. To declare their own innocence in the clash and persuade me I am guilty of failure and clumsiness. Which is nearly the same as incompetence. Which is almost the same as inefficiency. Which is practically the same as useless. Which is only one step away from total worthlessness.

Some days their voices win the game.

But not this day.

Not this time.

Angry spits of boiling water frothed out their messy spray across the stove top. Instinctively plunging a wooden spoon into the steaming mass I scooped the pasta concentrically inwards towards the centre, temporarily releasing it from the hot metal sides of the pan. Simultaneously my other hand rotated the stubby stove knob thirty degrees clockwise. The softening hiss of the gas flame was immediately drowned by the sound of manic grunts and screams.

Long hairy fibres on the draping sleeve of my cardigan burned and crackled. Shallow flames ran up my arm like a grass fire racing up the Pike on a hot Sunday in August. The sickly stink of singed wool infused uncomfortably with the smell of burning pasta. Gluten free. From the co-op. Swearing liberally at myself I doused the flames under the kitchen tap. The drowning flames chunnered soggy insults at me but I slapped them down. The part blackened pasta was green bin fodder but my bedraggled Irish wolf hound of a cardigan was washed, dried, shorn, worn and saved from the fire to live again.

The cardigan I can't remember

Young and not so young literary hopefuls politely shuffled their way around the perimeter of the U-shaped desks. Some had folders, others had notepads, one had a swanky looking tablet. Metal framed chair legs squeaked out their dreadful tuneless song across the wooden floor. They settled down for the second half of the workshop and I began to unpack our assignments for the afternoon. I gave them a choice of three writing exercises. One is poetry, one a short story, the other is a personal memoir.

My favourite of the three was the memoir because, not surprisingly, it's based around a cardigan. I'm braced for the incredulous giggles. "Think back to a time when someone hand knitted a cardigan for you? Who is/was that person to you? Can you picture the cardigan? Can you see that person knitting it especially with you in mind? Can you lean the ears of your heart back far enough through the years to perceive their distant expression of love for you, not in words, but in deeds?"

We explored the chronology of events which might precede the knitting of a cardigan for someone you love. My 'students' nodded politely. "Were you happy or embarrassed to wear a homemade item? Perhaps you were the knitter, can you describe that experience for me? Were you the shepherd who tended the sheep whose fleece eventually became the wool?"

Feeling pretty smug with what I saw as my irresistibly emotive and probing scene setting I prepared to hear all the lovely family stories about special mums, aunties and Grandmas. Those maternal ladies who sat in blissful companionship around the fire of an evening. Patiently working their craft, while listening to the 'wireless' or watching the box. I longed to know what wisdoms they exchanged, what china cups they drank their tea from and what kind of jam they spread on their homemade scones. How their garments turned out should certainly be recorded and surely the delightfully warm sepia fluffiness of their shared domestic experience must be written about.

No takers. Without exception everyone opted to work on the poetry exercise. I was gutted. Sulking was the only sensible option. Along with a gallon of tea in my recently gifted cup and saucer which strongly resembled a guzunda (goes under the bed). Five dunked custard creams duly set like mortar between my teeth before delivering a mind dulling sugar slump. Making it to the end of the workshop with enthusiasm was another effort of which I felt quite proud.

Arranging the chairs upside down on the desks I rethought my sales pitch about the home made cardigan. Switching off the classroom lights I headed for the bland municipal kitchen to wash up the mugs in the paradoxically tea stained, stainless steel sink. Putting them away inside a utilitarian cupboard typical of a certain era my parent's chunky birds eye maple sideboard came to mind.

Behind one of the ill-fitting doors of said sideboard stood a long pink cardboard tube bearing a photograph of a ladies corset, complete with four dangly bits for the attachment of stockings. Inside the tube were a selection of thin grey metal needles and two thick yellow plastic rods pointed at one tip and bluntly studded at the other. I liked that pair the best because the knitting grew faster. As a girl I had little patience and preferred sewing because it produced a quicker win. The soft focus memory of Mum patiently knitting and purling a cardigan with the thin grey needles occupies just a single frame in the 'nearly forgotten but not deleted' archive. In this fleeting faded mili-second of footage I also saw Mum hand stitching a 'fully fashioned' sleeve onto the front panel of a V-necked cardigan with four button holes. Sometimes I've doubted the truth of that memory, but there is a photograph which said to me: She did knit you a cardigan, the evidence is conclusive, you were loved, just believe it.

In Any Case

When you were young someone kept you warm and fed you. Maybe they held you in their arms and swaddled you up in a cardigan. Maybe they knitted it, maybe someone else did. In any case, you were loved beyond measure even though you couldn't know it. But that person who held you was just a person, like any other. They had limited time and limited energy and they couldn't be all that you needed them to be. Maybe they had their own troubles, with damage cutting deep into their own hearts. Maybe they didn't know how to demonstrate love very well. Maybe they actually couldn't demonstrate love very well. Maybe that person is still in your life, maybe they aren't. But, in any case, here is the message they would send for you.

My child

You were short changed, stitched up and ripped off. You didn't get the opportunities to shine that you so deserved to have. You didn't get the understanding, warmth, support and undivided attention which you so needed. You didn't get the affirmation and encouragement and praise that you had rightly earned. You weren't noticed enough. Seen enough. Heard enough. Held enough. In short you weren't loved and valued and cherished enough.

My fervent prayer is than one day you will truly believe way down deep in your heart, that I did my flat out level best for you. I was flawed and failed to deliver everything you needed, I admit it and I'm sorry. I hope that one day you will let go of the ill you feel towards me, let go of the hurt I know that I have caused you, either by design or default. I hope that one day you will really believe that I tried my very best, that I sacrificed much and gave you everything that I had to give, even though we both know that was not nearly enough.

If you choose to accept and believe it while you are this side of heaven, all the better, but if I have to wait until the other side where our true Father dwells, that will be fine with me too.

Though a vast ocean of light may separate us, know that I love you every single day, now and always. xxx

Biography

Val Fraser, aka Mrs Cardigan, has a background in journalism, marketing and communications and has written for numerous publications. She was formerly the Communications Officer for the Church of England Diocese of Liverpool before being invited to join United Christian Broadcasters (UCB) as their Creative Writer. She has worked on regional and national communications projects for clients which include the Diocese of Manchester, the Billy Graham Evangelical Association and Samaritan's Purse.

Val has written and directed several promotional videos and has penned the lyrics for three songs which have all been professionally recorded and performed.

Oh, and she loves cardigans!

Hellooo there fellow cardigan connoisseur :)

Thanks a shed-load for reading Life in Cardigans :) Let's not say goodbye just yet! For more cardigan stories, cardigan news and cardigan reviews join me at mrscardigan@blogspot.com.

Be great to see you there :)

Lightning Source UK Ltd.
Milton Keynes UK
UKOW06f0408310316

271231UK00009B/141/P